TAR FOR SMART PEOPLE

Expanded and Updated Second Edition

How Technology Assisted Review Works and Why
It Matters for Legal Professionals

John Tredennick | Mark Noel | Jeremy Pickens | Robert Ambrogi | Thomas C. Gricks III

"It is said that lawyers and judges went to law school because they were promised there would be no math. Their resistance to technological change is legendary. But, now, hell has frozen over. There is a book about TAR that is clear, incisive and actually fun to read. Lawyers now have no good reason to avoid understanding a technology which will transform discovery as nothing else has ever done."

-U.S. Magistrate Judge John M. Facciola (Retired)

AUTHORS

John Tredennick, Esq.

John Tredennick is the founder and chief executive officer of Catalyst. A nationally known trial lawyer and longtime litigation partner at Holland & Hart, John founded Catalyst in 2000 and is responsible for its overall direction, voice and vision. Well before founding Catalyst, John was a pioneer in the field of legal technology. He was editor-in-chief of the best-selling, multi-author, two-book series, *Winning With Computers: Trial Practice in the Twenty-First Century* (ABA Press 1990, 1991). At the same time, he wrote, *How to Prepare for Take and Use a Deposition at Trial* (James Publishing 1990), which he and his co-author continued to supplement for several years. He also wrote, *Lawyer's Guide to Spreadsheets* (Glasser Publishing 2000), and, *Lawyer's Guide to Microsoft Excel 2007* (ABA Press 2009).

John has been widely honored for his achievements. In 2013, he was named by *The American Lawyer* as one of the top six "E-Discovery Trailblazers" in their special issue on the "Top Fifty Big Law Innovators" in the past fifty years. In 2012, he was named to the FastCase 50, which recognizes the smartest, most courageous innovators, techies, visionaries and leaders in the law. London's *CityTech* magazine named him one of the "Top 100 Global Technology Leaders." In 2009, he was named the Ernst & Young Entrepreneur of the Year for Technology in the Rocky Mountain Region. Also in 2009, he was named the Top Technology Entrepreneur by the Colorado Software and Internet Association.

John is the former chair of the ABA's Law Practice Management Section. For many years, he was editor-in-chief of the ABA's *Law Practice Management* magazine. Over two decades, John has written scores of articles on legal technology and spoken on legal technology to audiences on four of the five continents.

Mark Noel, Esq.

Mark Noel is a managing director of professional services at Catalyst, where he specializes in helping clients use technology assisted review, advanced analytics and custom workflows to handle complex and large-scale litigations. Before joining Catalyst, Mark was a member of the Acuity team at FTI Consulting, co-founded an e-discovery software startup, and was an intellectual property litigator with Latham & Watkins LLP.

Mr. Noel graduated with honors from the University of Wisconsin Law School, and from the Georgia Institute of Technology with a degree in physics and minors in social and organizational psychology. Prior to law school, Mr. Noel was a researcher at Dartmouth College's Interactive Media Laboratory and Institute for Security Technology Studies, where his work focused on how people use technology to learn complex professional tasks.

Jeremy Pickens, Ph.D.

Jeremy Pickens is one of the world's leading information retrieval scientists and a pioneer in the field of collaborative exploratory search, a form of information seeking in which a group of people who share a common information need actively collaborate to achieve it. Dr. Pickens has seven patents and patents pending in the field of search and information retrieval.

As senior applied research scientist at Catalyst, Dr. Pickens has spearheaded the development of Insight Predict. His ongoing research and development focuses on methods for continuous learning, and the variety of real world technology assisted review workflows that are only possible with this approach.

Dr. Pickens earned his doctoral degree at the University of Massachusetts, Amherst, Center for Intelligent Information Retrieval. He conducted his post-doctoral work at King's College, London. Before joining Catalyst, he spent five years as a research scientist at FX Palo Alto Lab, Inc. In addition to his Catalyst responsibilities, he continues to organize research workshops and speak at scientific conferences around the world.

Robert Ambrogi, Esq.

A lawyer and veteran legal journalist, Bob serves as Catalyst's director of communications. He is also a practicing lawyer in Massachusetts and is the former editor-in-chief of *The National Law Journal*, *Lawyers USA* and *Massachusetts Lawyers Weekly*. A fellow of the College of Law Practice Management, he writes the award-winning blog *LawSites* and co-hosts the legal-affairs podcast *Lawyer2Lawyer*. He is a regular contributor to the *ABA Journal* and is vice chair of the editorial board of the ABA's *Law Practice* magazine.

Thomas C. Gricks III

A prominent e-discovery lawyer and one of the nation's leading authorities on the use of TAR in litigation, Tom is managing director, Professional Services, at Catalyst. He advises corporations and law firms on best practices for applying Catalyst's TAR technology, Insight Predict, to reduce the time and cost of discovery.

Tom has more than 25 years' experience as a trial lawyer and in-house counsel, most recently with the law firm Schnader Harrison Segal & Lewis, where he was a partner and chair of the e-Discovery Practice Group. He was lead e-discovery counsel in Global Aerospace v. Landow Aviation, the first case in the country to authorize the use of TAR over the objection of opposing counsel.

Tom's 2013 article, "The Implications of Rule 26(g) on the Use of Technology-Assisted Review," written with Karl Schieneman for The Federal Courts Law Review, is highly cited for its straightforward explanation of both the legal and technical underpinnings of TAR and its applications in litigation and discovery.

ISBN: 978-0-692-37565-5

To download the digital edition of this book, please visit:
www.catalystsecure.com/TARforSmartPeople

TABLE OF CONTENTS

Foreword

By Ralph Losey

Most technology lawyers know, or know of John Tredennick, and Catalyst, the company he started as a spin-off from his former law firm. But they may not know, as I do, how focused John and Catalyst are on creating the smartest AI-based predictive coding type search software possible. Adding TAR to your software is the right thing to do, the smart thing. Moreover, John is going about this in the right way. He is using a multi-disciplinary team approach to create this new predictive coding software. He has information scientists, computer engineers and tech-savvy lawyers from his company all working together. That is just the kind of approach I advocate in my *e-Discovery Team* blog.

Although John uses a multi-disciplinary team approach, he knows that this is a product designed for lawyers, not scientists. This book follows the same approach. Although scientific and engineering knowledge went into this book, it is written for lawyers and advanced paralegals. It avoids most of the over-technical jargon and scientific complexities. I am happy to recommend John's book to all legal professionals who want to learn more about predictive coding, and so take their search for evidence to the next level.

The continuous active learning (CAL) approach described in this book that does not utilize secret control sets, is definitively the way to go. I call it Predictive Coding 3.0, due to general industry evolution. It closely matches my writings on the subject and latest research. One of the best things about this book is all of the science that has gone into it. The book is informed by scientists, but written by a lawyer, a former trial lawyer at that, who is adept at explaining complex issues in a simple manner. That makes the science much more accessible to the legal community.

Sometimes simplifications of science can go too far and create distortions. That is another strength of this book, it was checked by a team of scientists and engineers at Catalyst for technical errors. The programmers at Catalyst try to follow the scientific research, not the other way around. That is the way it should be.

I found this to be an informative, current book on predictive coding. Although it is indeed written for smart people, not dummies, and has plenty of depth to it, the book avoids going into too many technical details. It is a good book for legal professionals who want to go beyond the simple introductions to predictive coding they may find elsewhere. As a lawyer himself, John understands the kind of knowledge that lawyers want and need to know about TAR. They will find it here. The smartest of the smart will be inspired to go further, and study the original source materials that John cites.

Ralph Losey is one of the world's leading experts on e-discovery law and practice. He is a shareholder in the national law firm Jackson Lewis P.C., where he leads the firm's Electronic Discovery practice group. He is also the author of the e-Discovery Team blog (www.e-discoveryteam.com) and publisher of the leading information resource, LegalSearchScience.com.

Since 2006, Ralph has limited his legal practice to electronic discovery and technology law. He has a special interest in software and the search and review of electronic evidence using artificial intelligence, and cybersecurity. Ralph has been involved with computers, software, legal hacking, and the law since 1980. He has presented at hundreds of legal conferences worldwide, written more than 500 articles, and published five books on electronic discovery. He is also the founder of Electronic Discovery Best Practices and founder and CEO of e-Discovery TeamTraining.

Introduction:

Second Edition

We published the first edition of *TAR for Smart People* in January 2015, just in time for LegalTech New York. As I wrote in the original introduction, the title was a play on the "For Dummies" series of books. In my experience in e-discovery, I haven't run into any dummies. So we addressed the book to all the smart people in the field.

In the year since, we have been surprised and encouraged by the positive reception the book has received. To be sure, we knew there were a lot of smart legal professionals out there looking to learn more about this important subject. What wasn't clear to us was whether they were ready for a book like this, focusing on the latest TAR 2.0 protocols in a straightforward but technically sophisticated manner.

I am pleased to report that the response to the book surpassed our expectations, leading us to publish this second, expanded and updated edition for LegalTech 2016. Indeed, the book has traveled farther and wider during its short life than I had imagined. We count readers from law firms, corporations and vendors across the United States as well as from Asia and the EU.

Tar for Smart People has been used as a text for a number of e-discovery courses helping law students learn about this important subject. Judges from both federal and state courts have used it at judicial conferences to help their colleagues get up to speed on the latest TAR methods. Practitioners from some of the largest and most prestigious law firms in the world have told me they keep it on their desks for reference.

More importantly, over the past year, TAR 2.0 and its continuous active learning (CAL) protocol moved from industry upstart to broad recognition as the de facto standard for predictive analytics. The ball started rolling in 2014 when attorney Maura Grossman and Professor Gordon Cormack published landmark research demonstrating the superiority of CAL over earlier TAR 1.0 protocols. Momentum grew as other scientists showed similar results across hundreds of cases, with CAL beating one-time training every time.

Today, savvy TAR users understand the cost savings and time benefits of CAL over one-time training. They also appreciate the practical benefits of this newer protocol. These include the ability to handle rolling collections, to have reviewers rather than senior lawyers do training, and an uncanny ability to find relevant documents when collection richness is low.

This second edition of *TAR for Smart People* adds several new chapters, including one to help you ask your TAR vendor the right questions about CAL, along with several new case studies that further reinforce the power of TAR 2.0 systems over first-generation TAR tools. We also update TAR case law so you have the latest decisions at your fingertips. Lastly, we have taken comments from our readers and updated or clarified sections that needed improvement. We worked hard to make this important subject comprehensible but there is always room to improve.

If you read the first edition of this book, we hope you will enjoy the new content we have added. If you have not seen the book, then we hope you enjoy this second edition of *TAR for Smart People* even more. The subject is vital for all e-discovery professionals who are interested in lowering the total cost of review. There is simply no easier or more obvious way to cut review costs out there.

TAR for dummies? It turns out there were a lot more smart people out there after all.

–John Tredennick, Esq.
Founder and CEO, Catalyst

Introduction:

TAR for Smart People

We've all seen the "For Dummies" series of explanatory books. But in the e-discovery field, I haven't run into many dummies. To the contrary, the lawyers and other professionals I meet are pretty darn smart. For that reason, when we conceived of producing this book about technology assisted review (TAR), we decided to write it for all the smart people working in this field.

Just because a legal professional is smart doesn't mean he or she fully understands TAR. Rather, TAR is a sophisticated and highly developed process which draws on science, technology and law. There are many different approaches to it and a lot to learn before you can master the subject.

At bottom, TAR systems share two common characteristics. One is that they leverage human knowledge through technology to find relevant documents more quickly and with less effort. The other is that they produce savings in review time and costs, although some do this much better than others.

How Does it Work?

The simple way to understand how TAR works is to think of it like the Pandora Internet radio service. Pandora has millions of songs in its archive but no idea what kind of music you like. Its goal is to play music from your favorite artists but also to present new songs you might like.

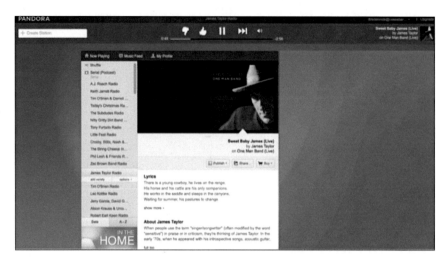

How does Pandora do this? For those who haven't tried it, you start by giving Pandora the name of one or more artists you like, thus creating a "station." Pandora begins by playing a song or two by the artists you have selected. Then, it chooses a similar song or artist you didn't select to see if you like it. You answer by clicking a "thumbs up" or "thumbs down" button. Information retrieval (IR) scientists call this "relevance feedback."

Pandora analyzes the songs you like, as well as the songs you don't, to make its suggestions. It looks at factors such as melody, harmony, rhythm, form, composition and lyrics to find similar songs. As you give it feedback on its suggestions, it uses that information tomake better selections the next time. The IR people would call this"training."

The process continues as you listen to your radio station. The more feedback you provide, the smarter the system gets. The end result is Pandora plays a lot of music you like and, occasionally, something you don't like.

TAR: Simple but Not for Dummies

TAR is a lot like Pandora, only you work with documents rather than songs. As you train the system, it gets smarter about which documents are relevant to your inquiry, and which are not. It is as simple as that.

To date, every court that has considered TAR has approved it as a reasonable approach to find relevant documents and determine which documents do not require review. Indeed, in a recent decision federal Magistrate-Judge Peck declared that "the case law has developed to the point that it is now black letter law that where the producing party wants to utilize TAR for document review, courts will permit it." [1]

To be sure, there remains debate over differing TAR protocols and, in particular, how much information about the training process has to be shared. However, there are few who question the efficacy and cost savings inherent in the TAR process itself. TAR is here to stay and is well worth learning about.

In the chapters that follow, we will provide an introduction to TAR and then dig deeper into some of the key issues surrounding the process. We'll look at different TAR protocols, especially the newest and most-promising protocol, continuous active learning.

We'll explore the different schools of thought about important TAR issues such as the best use of subject matter experts and the need for random sampling. We'll also cover various uses of TAR you may not know about, and conclude with some actual case studies showing TAR's effectiveness in practice.

This isn't a book for dummies. This book confronts some difficult questions surrounding TAR and explores them in some depth. Not everyone will agree with everything we say here. At the very least, however, we hope this book will help you refine your understanding of the process and make even smarter decisions about it going forward.

–John Tredennick, Esq.
Founder and CEO, Catalyst

1. *Rio Tinto PLC v. Vale SA*, Case 1:14-cv-03042-RMB-AJP (S.D. N.Y. March 3, 2015).

1

Introduction to Technology Assisted Review

Technology assisted review (TAR), aka predictive coding, predictive ranking, or computer assisted review, is a process whereby humans interact with a computer to find relevant documents. Just as there are many names for the process, there are many different approaches to it. At bottom, however, all of these systems leverage human knowledge about relevant documents to find more potentially relevant documents.

The process is interactive. A human reviews and tags a document as relevant or non-relevant. The computer takes the human input and uses it to draw inferences about other documents. Ultimately, the computer orders the documents by relevance to guide the review process. Humans then decide how many documents need to be reviewed.

Savings are what make TAR interesting, if not revolutionary. Review teams can work faster using prioritized (ordered) review because they are reviewing documents with similar content. Clients save on review costs because TAR provides a reasonable basis to "cut off" review once most of the relevant documents have been found.

The savings in review time and costs for a successful TAR project are substantial, which is why the topic is important. (In some cases TAR allows you to remove 95% or even more documents from the review.) You defend the decision to cut off review through relatively simple sampling techniques, which show your success in promoting relevant documents to the top of the stack and prove that the documents left behind are mostly non-relevant.

Understanding How TAR Works

As we said in the introduction, TAR works in a similar way to Pandora, only you work with documents rather than songs. As you train the system, it gets smarter about which documents are relevant to your inquiry and which are not.[1] It is as simple as that.

Of course, TAR involves more serious matters than simple music choice, so there are a few more options and strategies to consider. Also, different vendors approach the process in different ways, which can cause some confusion. But here is a start toward explaining the process.

1. **Collect the documents you want to review and feed them to the computer.**

    To start, the computer has to analyze the documents you want to review (or not review), just like Pandora needs to analyze all the music it maintains. While approaches vary, most systems analyze the words in your documents in terms of frequency in the document and across the population.

    Some systems require that you collect all of the documents before you begin training. Others, like Insight Predict, allow you to add documents during the training process. Different approaches can work but some are more efficient and easy to administer than others.

2. **Start training/review.**

    You have two choices here. You can start by presenting documents you know are relevant (or non-relevant) to the computer or you can let the computer select documents randomly for your consideration. With Pandora, you start by identifying an artist you like. This gives the computer a headstart on your preferences. In theory, you could let Pandora select music randomly to see if you liked it but this would be pretty inefficient.

Either way, you begin by giving the computer examples of which documents you like (relevant) and which you don't like (non-relevant).[2] From these examples, the system learns more about your preferences—which terms tend to occur in relevant documents and which in non-relevant ones. It then develops a mathematical formula to help it predict the relevance of other documents in the population.

There is an ongoing debate about whether training requires the examples to be provided by subject matter experts (SMEs) to be effective. Our research (and that of others) suggests that review teams assisted by SMEs are just as effective as SMEs alone. Others disagree. You can read more about this issue later in this book.

3. Rank the documents by relevance.

This is the heart of the process. Based on the training you have provided, the system creates a formula that it uses to rank (order) your documents by estimated relevance.

4. Continue training/review (rinse and repeat).

Continue training using your SME or review team. Many systems will suggest additional documents for training, which will help the algorithm get better at understanding your document population. This is called "Active" learning. For the most part, the more training/review you do, the better the system will be at ranking the unseen documents.

5. Test the ranking.

How good a job did the system do on the ranking? If the ranking is "good enough," move forward and finish your review. If it is not, continue your training.

Some systems view training as a process separate from review. Following this approach, your SMEs would handle the training until they were satisfied that the algorithm was fully trained. They would then let the review teams look at the higher-ranked documents, possibly discarding those below a certain threshold as non-relevant.

Our research suggests that a continuous learning process is more effective. We therefore recommend that you feed reviewer judgments back to the system for a process of continuous learning. As a result, the algorithm continues to get smarter, which can mean even fewer documents need to be reviewed. You can read more about this issue later in this book.

6. Finish the review.

The end goal is to finish the review as efficiently and cost-effectively as possible. In a linear review, you typically review all of the documents in the population. In a predictive review, you can stop well before then because the important documents have been moved to the front of the queue. You save on both review costs and the time it takes to complete the review.

Ultimately, "finishing" means reviewing down the ranking until you have found enough relevant documents, with the concept of proportionality taking center stage. Thus, you may stop after reviewing the first 20% of the ranking because you have found 80% of the relevant documents. Your argument is that the cost to review the remaining 80% of the document population just to find the remaining 20% of the relevant documents is unduly burdensome.[3]

That's all there is to it. While there are innumerable choices in applying the process to a real case, the rest is just strategy and execution.

How Do I Know if the Process is Successful?

That, of course, is the million-dollar question. Fortunately, the answer is relatively easy.

The process succeeds to the extent that the document ranking places more relevant documents at the front of the pack than you might get when the documents are ordered by other means (e.g. by date or Bates number). How successful you are depends on the degree to which the predictive ranking is better than what you might get using your traditional approach.

Let me offer an example. Imagine your documents are represented by a series of cells, as in the below diagram. The shaded cells represent relevant documents and the white cells non-relevant.

What we have is essentially a random distribution, or at least there is no discernable pattern between relevant and non-relevant. In that regard, this might be similar to a review case where you ordered documents by Bates number or date. In most cases, there is no reason to expect that relevant documents would appear at the front of the order.

This is typical of a linear review. If you review 10% of the documents, you likely will find 10% of the relevant documents. If you review 50%, you will likely find 50% of the relevant documents.

Take a look at this next diagram. It represents the outcome of a perfect ordering. The relevant documents come first followed by non-relevant documents.

If you could be confident that the ranking worked perfectly, as in this example, it is easy to see the benefit of ordering by rank. Rather than review all of the documents to find relevant ones, you could simply review the first 20% and be done. You could confidently ignore the remaining 80% (perhaps after sampling them) or, at least, direct them to a lower-priced review team.

Yes, but What Is the Ranking Really Like?

Since this is directed at smart people, I am sure you realize that computer rankings are never that good. At the same time, they are rarely (if ever) as bad as you might see in a linear review.

Following our earlier examples, here is how the actual ranking might look using predictive ranking:

We see that the algorithm certainly improved on the random distribution, although it is far from perfect. We have 30% of the relevant documents at the top of the order, followed by an increasing mix of non-relevant documents. At about a third of the way into the review, you would start to run out of relevant documents.

This would be a success by almost any measure. If you stopped your review at the midway point, you would have seen all but one relevant document. By cutting out half the document population, you would save substantially on review costs.

How Do I Measure Success?

If the goal of TAR is to arrange a set of documents in order of likely relevance to a particular issue, the measure of success is the extent to which you meet that goal. Put as a question: "Am I getting more relevant documents at the start of my review than I might with my typical approach (often a linear review)."[4] If the answer is yes, then how much better?

To answer these questions, we need to take two additional steps. First, for comparison purposes, we will want to measure the "richness" of the overall document population. Second, we need to determine how effective our ranking system turned out to be against the entire document population.

1. **Estimating richness:** Richness is a measure of how many relevant documents are in your total document population. Some people call this "prevalence," as a reference to how prevalent relevant documents are in the total population. For example, we might estimate that 15% or the documents are relevant, with 85% non-relevant. Or we might say document prevalence is 15%.

    How do we estimate richness? Once the documents are assembled, we can use random sampling for this purpose. In general, a random sample allows us to look at a small subset of the document population, and make predictions about the nature of the larger set.[5] Thus, from the example above, if our sample found 15 documents out of a hundred to be relevant, we would project a richness of 15%. Extrapolating that to the larger population (100,000 for example), we might estimate that there were about 15,000 relevant documents to be found.

For those really smart people who understand statistics, I am skipping a discussion about confidence intervals and margins of error. Let me just say that the larger the sample size, the more confident you can be in your estimate. But, surprisingly, the sample size does not have to be that large to provide a high degree of confidence. You can read more about this topic later in this book.

2. **Evaluating the ranking:** Once the documents are ranked, we can then sample the ranking to determine how well our algorithm did in pushing relevant documents to the top of the stack. We do this through a systematic random sample.

In a systematic random sample, we sample the documents in their ranked order, tagging them as relevant or non-relevant as we go. Specifically, we sample every Nth document from the top to the bottom of the ranking (e.g. every 100th document). Using this method helps ensure that we are looking at documents across the ranking spectrum, from highest to lowest.

As an aside, you can actually use a systematic random sample to determine overall richness/prevalence and to evaluate the ranking. Unless you need an initial richness estimate, say for review planning purposes, we recommend you do both steps at the same time.

Comparing the Results

We can compare the results of the systematic random sample to the richness of our population by plotting what scientists call a "yield curve." While this may sound daunting, it is really rather simple. It is the one diagram you should know about if you are going to use TAR.

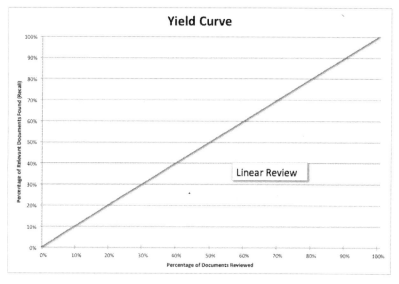

A yield curve can be used to show the progress of a review and the results it yields, at least in number of relevant documents found. The X-axis shows the percentage of documents to be reviewed (or reviewed). The Y-axis shows the percentage of relevant documents found (or you would expect to find) at any given point in the review.

Linear Review: Knowing that the document population is 15% rich (give or take) provides a useful baseline against which we can measure the success of our predictive ranking effort. We plot richness as a diagonal line going from zero to 100%. It reflects the fact that, in a linear review, we expect the percentage of relevant documents to correlate to the percentage of total documents reviewed.

Following that notion, we can estimate that if the team were to review 10% of the document population, they would likely see 10% of the relevant documents. If they were to look at 50% of the documents, we would expect them to find 50% of the relevant documents, give or take. If they wanted to find 80% of the relevant documents, they would have to look at 80% of the entire population.

Predictive Review: Now let's plot the results of our systematic random sample. The purpose is to show how the review might progress if we reviewed documents in a ranked order, from likely relevant to likely non-relevant. We can easily compare it to a linear review to measure the success of the predictive ranking process.

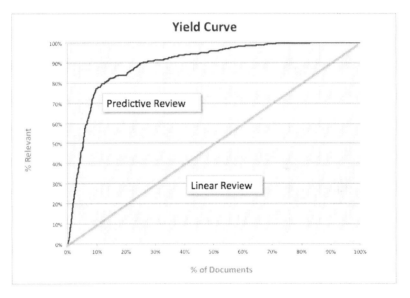

You can quickly see that the line for the Predictive Review goes up more steeply than the one for linear review. This reflects the fact that in a Predictive Review the team starts with the most likely relevant documents. The line continues to rise until you hit the 80% relevant mark, which happens after a review of about 10-12% of the entire document population. The slope then flattens, particularly as you cross the 90% relevant line. That reflects the fact that you won't find as many relevant documents from that point onward. Put another way, you will have to look through a lot more documents before you find your next relevant one.

We now have what we need to measure the success of our predictive ranking project. To recap, we needed:

1. A richness estimate so we have an idea of how many relevant documents are in the population.

2. A systematic random sample so we can estimate how many relevant documents got pushed to the front of the ordering.

It is now relatively easy to quantify success. As the yield curve illustrates, if I engage in a Predictive Review, I will find about 80% of the relevant documents after only reviewing about 12% of total documents. If I wanted to review 90% of the relevant documents, I could stop after reviewing just over 20% of the population. My measure of success would be the savings achieved over a linear review.

At this point we move into proportionality arguments. What is the right stopping point for our case? The answer depends on the needs of your case, the nature of the documents and any stipulated protocols among the parties. At the least, the yield curve helps you frame the argument in a meaningful way.

Footnotes

1. IR specialists call these documents "relevant" but they do not mean relevant in a legal sense. They mean important to your inquiry even though you may not plan on introducing them at trial. You could substitute "hot," "responsive," "privileged" or some other criterion depending on the nature of your review.

2. We could use "irrelevant" but that has a different shade of meaning for the IR people so I bow to their use of non-relevant here. Either word works for this discussion.

3. Sometimes at the meet-and-confer, the parties agree on predictive ranking protocols, including the percentage of relevant documents that need to be found in the review.

4. We will use a linear review (essentially a random relevance ordering) as a baseline because that is the way most reviews are done. If you review based on conceptual clusters or some other method, your baseline for comparison would be different.

5. Note that an estimate based on a random sample is not valid unless you are sampling against the entire population. If you get new documents, you have to redo your sample.

2

A Brief History of Technology Assisted Review

Technology assisted review is now so widely used in e-discovery and so widely accepted by judges that one federal magistrate-judge recently declared it to be "black letter law." But it was only three years earlier when that same judge, Andrew J. Peck, issued the first decision ever to approve the use of TAR. And it has been just five years since the terms TAR and predictive coding first began to filter into the legal profession's vernacular.

So how did TAR take root among lawyers? And how did it become so widespread so quickly?

Neither question has an easy answer. For TAR, there was no "Mr. Watson, come here!" moment of invention. Rather, TAR developed and took hold gradually at first, as understanding grew that it offered a viable solution for spiraling litigation costs driven by rapidly escalating quantities of data in litigation.

Tracing TAR's Roots

One of the earliest articles to describe anything akin to TAR was by

Anne Kershaw in 2005, "Automated Document Review Proves Its Reliability." [1] She described a study she conducted that compared a human review team against an automated document assessment system. While the humans identified only 51% of relevant documents, the automated system identified more than 95% percent.

The technology her article described was not what we think of today as TAR or predictive coding. But it similarly used statistical techniques to determine which documents were relevant and her analysis foreshadowed TAR's eventual refinement.

"Automated document review and analysis provides significant new opportunities for attorneys in law firms and in corporate legal departments," Kershaw wrote. "Legal review can be a more efficient, less costly, and a more proactive process that aids the legal team in managing the case."

A key step forward came in 2006. That year, the Text Retrieval Conference, an organization started in 1992 by the National Institute of Standards and Technology (NIST) and the U.S. Department of Defense to study information retrieval techniques, launched the TREC Legal Track devoted to the use of search and information retrieval in law. Its annual research projects provided (and continue to provide) critical evidence of the efficacy of these techniques in e-discovery.

TAR Enters the Vernacular

It is impossible to pinpoint when any of the names we now use for this process—not just TAR, but also "computer-assisted review" and "predictive coding"—first came into use. They are mentioned nowhere in the TREC studies from 2006 to 2010. They are also nowhere to be found in another seminal early guide, The *Sedona Conference Best Practices Commentary on the Use of Search and Information Retrieval Methods in E-Discovery*, published in 2007. A 2006 CLE handout [2] referenced "machine-assisted review."

What is clear, however, is that by 2010, these concepts had entered the legal profession's vernacular. In fact, the years 2010 to 2013 were the critical juncture in the growth of TAR, with a series of developments that signaled that this evolving technology deserved serious attention.

The first of these developments was the 2010 publication of a study comparing the results of computer-assisted review to manual review. The study, "Document Categorization in Legal Electronic Discovery: Computer Classification vs. Manual Review," [3] was conducted by Kershaw along with Herbert L. Roitblat and Patrick Oot, who were all at the time affiliated with the Electronic Discovery Institute.

The study challenged the conventional wisdom that human review is the gold standard. It sought to determine "whether there was a benefit to engaging a traditional human review or whether computer systems could be relied on to produce comparable results." Their conclusion: "On every measure, the performance of the two computer systems was at least as accurate (measured against the original review) as that of human re-review."

Two Key Developments

A year later, another study even further upset the conventional wisdom. Two e-discovery researchers, Maura R. Grossman, counsel at Wachtell, Lipton, Rosen & Katz, and Gordon V. Cormack, co-director of the Information Retrieval Group at the University of Waterloo, analyzed data from the 2009 TREC Legal Track involving the use of TAR processes. They concluded that TAR was not only more effective than human review at finding relevant documents, but also much cheaper.

"Overall, the myth that exhaustive manual review is the most effective—and therefore the most defensible—approach to document review is strongly refuted," they wrote in the *Richmond Journal of Law and Technology* [4]. "Technology-assisted review can (and does) yield more accurate results than exhaustive manual review, with much lower effort." Their study found that TAR produced a 50-fold savings in cost over manual review.

For lawyers and clients facing spiraling e-discovery costs, this was big news. It provided evidence that TAR could be both more effective than manual review and also significantly cheaper. But even with this evidence, many lawyers still saw one big obstacle to using TAR: the uncertainty of its acceptability to the courts.

That obstacle was significantly lowered on Feb. 24, 2012, when Judge Peck issued his opinion endorsing the use of TAR in a case pending before him, *Da Silva Moore v. Publicis Groupe*.[5] It was the first judicial opinion anywhere to endorse the use of TAR. "Computer-assisted review appears to be better than the available alternatives, and thus should be used in appropriate cases," he wrote, opening the door to a sea change in how lawyers conduct e-discovery.

The second major milestone in the courts came just two months later with the case *Global Aerospace, Inc. v. Landow Aviation, L.P.*, No. CL 61040 (Vir. Cir. Ct. Apr. 23, 2012). *In Da Silva Moore*, the court approved TAR based on the parties' agreement. *Global Aerospace* was the first case to approve the use of TAR over the opponent's objection. It was also the first state court case to approve the use of TAR.

(A contributing author to this book, Thomas Gricks, was lead e-discovery counsel in *Global Aerospace*. His work on that case was highlighted in a 2013 *Wall Street Journal* article, "How a Computer Did the Work of Many Lawyers." [6])

The Evolving Capabilities of TAR

There remained one factor limiting TAR's widespread adoption—the limits of the technology itself. While first-generation TAR systems (TAR 1.0) represented a major—indeed, revolutionary—advance over manual review and keyword searching, they had shortcomings that limited their usefulness in many real-world contexts.

For one, TAR 1.0 systems required that a senior attorney be involved in training the system. The senior attorney would have to review and code hundreds or thousands of random documents until the system stabilized. Given that the goal of TAR was to reduce costs, requiring the involvement of a senior attorney was not a cost-effective way to go about it. In addition, requiring involvement of a senior attorney also frequently delayed the process from ever getting started in the first place.

Another shortcoming of TAR 1.0 systems was that they required legal teams to have all their documents at the start. If a subsequent batch of documents arrived later, as is typical in practice, the training would have to begin all over again.

Those shortcomings were overcome with the development of a new generation of TAR systems—so-called TAR 2.0 systems. Now gaining wide popularity, these newer systems no longer require senior attorneys for training. Instead, through a process known as "continuous active learning," the review team can simply begin reviewing documents and the system will continuously learn from their coding calls and improve its results.

Also, because the system is continually learning and refreshing its rankings, new documents can be added at any time. This conforms to the way litigation occurs in the real world, where discovery documents typically arrive on a rolling basis.

In a 2014 peer-reviewed controlled study, *Evaluation of Machine-Learning Protocols for Technology-Assisted Review in Electronic Discovery*,[7] Grossman and Cormack documented the superiority of CAL systems over earlier forms of TAR. Their study found that CAL yielded "generally superior results" to other TAR systems and required "substantially and significantly less human review effort."

TAR's History Continues

Five years ago, TAR was virtually unheard of in litigation. Today, it has become essential litigation technology for its ability to prioritize documents and reduce the time and cost of review. Last year, more than half of U.S. corporations reported using TAR in litigation. There can be no doubt that percentage will continue to grow.

The history of TAR is still taking shape. But its place in the legal industry is now firmly embedded.

Footnotes

1. Anne Kershaw, *Automated Document Review Proves Its Reliability*, Digital Discovery & e-Evidence, Volume 5, Number 11, http://www.akershaw.com/Documents/2004AEKDocReviewArticle.pdf.

2. Patrick Oot, Sonya L. Sigler & Miriam M. Smolen, *Leading Through the Electronic Discovery Quagmire (Part 1): Nuts & Bolts Best Practices*, Association of Corporate Counsel 2006 Annual Meeting, http://www.acc.com/vl/public/ProgramMaterial/loader.cfm?csModule=security/getfile&pageid=20150&title=untitled&recorded=1.

3. Herbert L. Roitblat, Anne Kershaw & Patrick Oot, *Document Categorization in Legal Electronic Discovery: Computer Classification vs. Manual Review*, Journal of the American Society for Information Science and Technology, 61(1):1–11, 2010.

4. Maura R. Grossman & Gordon V. Cormack, *Technology-Assisted Review in E-Discovery Can Be More Effective and More Efficient Than Exhaustive Manual Review*, XVII RICH. J.L. & TECH. 11 (2011), http://jolt.richmond.edu/v17i3/article11.pdf.

5. *Da Silva Moore, et al. v. Publicis Groupe*, No. 11 Civ. 1279 (ALC)(AJP), 2012 WL 607412 (S.D.N.Y. Feb. 24, 2012).

6. http://blogs.wsj.com/law/2013/01/17/how-a-computer-did-the-work-of-many-lawyers/.

7. Gordon V. Cormack & Maura R. Grossman, *Evaluation of Machine Learning Protocols for Technology-Assisted Review in Electronic Discovery*, in Proceedings of the 37th International ACM SIGIR Conference on Research and Development in Information Retrieval (SIGIR '14) (July 2014), at 153-62, http://dx.doi. org/10.1145/2600428.2609601.

3

How Much Can CAL Save?

A Closer Look at the Grossman/ Cormack Research Results

As we explained in the last chapter, in 2014, two leading experts in technology assisted review, Maura R. Grossman and Gordon V. Cormack, presented the first peer-reviewed scientific study on the effectiveness of several TAR protocols, "Evaluation of Machine-Learning Protocols for Technology-Assisted Review in Electronic Discovery".

Perhaps the most important conclusion of the study was that an advanced TAR 2.0 protocol, continuous active learning (CAL), proved to be far more effective than the two standard TAR 1.0 protocols used by most of the early products on the market today—simple passive learning (SPL) and simple active learning (SAL).

To quote Grossman and Cormack:

> *"The results show that entirely non-random training methods, in which the initial training documents are selected using a simple keyword search, and subsequent training documents are selected by active learning [CAL], require substantially and*

significantly less human review effort . . . to achieve any given level of recall, than passive learning, in which the machine-learning algorithm plays no role in the selection of training documents [SPL]. ...

Among active-learning methods, continuous active learning with relevance feedback yields generally superior results to simple active learning with uncertainty sampling [SAL], while avoiding the vexing issue of "stabilization"—determining when training is adequate, and therefore may stop."

But how much can you expect to save using CAL over the simple passive and active learning methods used by TAR 1.0 programs? While every case is different, as are the algorithms that different vendors employ, we can draw some interesting conclusions from the Grossman/Cormack study that will help answer this question.

Comparing CAL with SPL and SAL

Grossman and Cormack compared the three TAR protocols against eight different matters. Four were from an earlier Text REtrieval Conference (TREC) program and four were from actually litigated cases.

After charting the results from each matter, they offered summary information about their results. In this case I will show them for a typical TAR 1.0 project with 2,000 training seeds.

Comparing CAL to SPL and SAL with 2,000 Training Seeds				
Matter	Collection Size	CAL	SPL	SAL
201	723,537	6,000	284,000	237,000
202	723,537	11,000	47,000	34,000
203	723,537	6,000	521,000	43,000
207	723,537	11,000	103,000	55,000
A	1,118,116	11,000	502,000	210,000
B	409,277	8,000	142,000	119,000
C	293,549	4,000	9,000	5,000
D	405,796	18,000	55,000	60,000

A quick visual inspection confirms that the CAL protocol requires the review of far fewer documents than required for simple passive or simple active learning. In Matter 201, for example, a CAL review requires inspection of 6,000 documents in order to find 75% of the relevant files. In sharp contrast, reviewers using a SPL protocol would have to view 284,000 documents. For SAL, they would have to review almost as many, 237,000 documents. Both TAR 1.0 protocols require review of more than 230,000 documents. At $4 per document for review and QC, the extra cost from using the TAR 1.0 protocols would come to almost a million dollars.

Clearly some of the other matters had numbers that were much closer. Matter C, for example, required the review of 4,000 for a CAL protocol but only 5,000 for SAL and 9,000 for SPL. In such a case, the savings are much smaller, hardly justifying a switch in TAR applications. So what might we expect as a general rule if we were considering different approaches to TAR?

Averaging the Results Across Matters

Lacking more comparative data, one way to answer this question is to use the averages across all eight matters to make our analysis.

Comparing CAL to SPL and SAL with 2,000 Training Seeds				
Matter	Collection Size	CAL	SPL	SAL
201	723,537	6,000	284,000	237,000
202	723,537	11,000	47,000	34,000
203	723,537	6,000	521,000	43,000
207	723,537	11,000	103,000	55,000
A	1,118,116	11,000	502,000	210,000
B	409,277	8,000	142,000	119,000
C	293,549	4,000	9,000	5,000
D	405,796	18,000	55,000	60,000
Average	640,111	9,375	207,875	95,375

Our average matter size is just over 640,000. The CAL protocol would require review of 9,375 documents. With SPL you would have to review 207,875 documents. With SAL, you would only have to review 95,375 documents. Clearly SAL is to be preferred to SPL but it still required the review of an extra 86,000 documents.

How much would that cost? To determine this there are several factors to consider. First, the TAR 1.0 protocols require that a subject matter expert do the initial training. CAL does not require this. Thus, we have to determine the hourly rate of the SME. We then have to determine how many documents an hour the expert (and later the reviewers) can get through. Lastly, we have to have an estimate for reviewer costs.

Here are some working assumptions:

1. Cost for a subject matter expert: $350/hour.

2. Cost for a standard reviewer: $60/hour.

3. Documents per hour reviewed (for both SME and reviewer): 60.

If we use these assumptions and work against our matter averages, we find this information about the costs of using the three protocols. On an average review, at least based on these eight matters, you can expect to save over a quarter million dollars in review costs if you use CAL as your TAR protocol. You can expect to save $115,000 over a simple active learning system. These are significant sums.

Comparing CAL to SPL and SAL with 2,000 Training Seeds				
Matter	Collection Size	CAL	SPL	SAL
201	723,537	6,000	284,000	237,000
202	723,537	11,000	47,000	34,000
203	723,537	6,000	521,000	43,000
207	723,537	11,000	103,000	55,000
A	1,118,116	11,000	502,000	210,000
B	409,277	8,000	142,000	119,000
C	293,549	4,000	9,000	5,000
D	405,796	18,000	55,000	60,000
Average	640,111	9,375	207,875	95,375
Reviewed by SME			2,000	2,000
Expert review cost			$11,667	$11,667
Reviewer cost		$11,719	$257,344	$116,719
Total review cost		$11,719	$269,010	$128,385

What About Using More Training Seeds?

As I mentioned earlier, Grossman and Cormack reported the results when substantially more training seeds were used: 5,000 and 8,000. If your subject matter expert is willing to review substantially more training documents, the cost savings from using CAL is less. However, at 60 documents an hour, your SME will spend 83 hours (about two weeks) doing the training with 5,000 seeds. He/she will spend more than 133 hours (about 3.5 weeks) if you go for 8,000 seeds. Even worse, he/she may have to redo the training if new documents come in later.

That said, here is how the numbers worked out for 5,000 training seeds.

Comparison of CAL to SPL and SAL with 5,000 Training Seeds				
Matter	Collection Size	CAL	SPL (5,000)	SAL (5,000)
201	723,537	6,000	331,000	7,000
202	723,537	11,000	29,000	12,000
203	723,537	6,000	331,000	7,000
207	723,537	11,000	50,000	23,000
A	1,118,116	11,000	326,000	42,000
B	409,277	8,000	41,000	10,000
C	293,549	4,000	8,000	8,000
D	405,796	18,000	38,000	54,000
Average	640,111	9,375	144,250	20,375
Reviewed by SME			5,000	5,000
Expert review cost			$29,167	$29,167
Reviewer cost		$11,719	$174,063	$19,219
Total review cost		$11,719	$203,229	$48,385
Savings from CAL			$191,510	$36,667

And for 8,000 training seeds.

Comparison of CAL to SPL and SAL with 8,000 Training Seeds				
Matter	Collection Size	CAL	SPL (8,000)	SAL (8,000)
201	723,537	6,000	164,000	10,000
202	723,537	11,000	26,000	14,000
203	723,537	6,000	154,000	10,000
207	723,537	11,000	36,000	13,000
A	1,118,116	11,000	204,000	12,000
B	409,277	8,000	21,000	11,000
C	293,549	4,000	10,000	10,000
D	405,796	18,000	37,000	53,000
Average	640,111	9,375	81,500	16,625
Reviewed by SME			8,000	8,000
Expert review cost			$46,667	$46,667
Reviewer cost		$11,719	$91,875	$10,781
Total review cost		$11,719	$138,542	$57,448
Savings from CAL			$126,823	$45,729

The first thing to note is that the number of documents that ultimately have to be reviewed reduces as you add more training seeds. This seems logical and supports the fundamental CAL notion that the more training seeds you give to the algorithm the better the results. However, also note that the total review cost for SAL increases as you go from 5,000 to 8,000 training seeds. This is because we assume you have to pay more for SME training than review team training. With CAL, the reviewers do the training.

How Much Time Can I Save?

So far, we have only spoken about cost savings. What about time savings? We can quickly see how much time the CAL protocol saves as well.

For 2,000 training seeds:

Comparing CAL to SPL and SAL with 2,000 Training Seeds				
Matter	Collection Size	CAL	SPL	SAL
201	723,537	6,000	284,000	237,000
202	723,537	11,000	47,000	34,000
203	723,537	6,000	521,000	43,000
207	723,537	11,000	103,000	55,000
A	1,118,116	11,000	502,000	210,000
B	409,277	8,000	142,000	119,000
C	293,549	4,000	9,000	5,000
D	405,796	18,000	55,000	60,000
Average	640,111	9,375	207,875	95,375
Reviewed by SME			2,000	2,000
Review time (hours)		156	3,465	1,590
Time savings (hours)			3,308	1,433

For 5,000 training seeds:

Comparison of CAL to SPL and SAL with 8,000 Training Seeds				
Matter	Collection Size	CAL	SPL (8,000)	SAL (8,000)
201	723,537	6,000	164,000	10,000
202	723,537	11,000	26,000	14,000
203	723,537	6,000	154,000	10,000
207	723,537	11,000	36,000	13,000
A	1,118,116	11,000	204,000	12,000
B	409,277	8,000	21,000	11,000
C	293,549	4,000	10,000	10,000
D	405,796	18,000	37,000	53,000
Average	640,111	9,375	81,500	16,625
Reviewed by SME			8,000	8,000
Review time (hours)		156	1,358	277
Time savings (hours)			1,202	121

And, for 8,000 training seeds:

Comparison of CAL to SPL and SAL with 5,000 Training Seeds				
Matter	Collection Size	CAL	SPL (5,000)	SAL (5,000)
201	723,537	6,000	331,000	7,000
202	723,537	11,000	29,000	12,000
203	723,537	6,000	331,000	7,000
207	723,537	11,000	50,000	23,000
A	1,118,116	11,000	326,000	42,000
B	409,277	8,000	41,000	10,000
C	293,549	4,000	8,000	8,000
D	405,796	18,000	38,000	54,000
Average	640,111	9,375	144,250	20,375
Reviewed by SME			5,000	5,000
Review time (hours)		156	2,404	340
Time savings (hours)			2,248	183

As with cost savings, there are substantial review time savings to be had using CAL over simple passive learning and simple active learning. The savings range from 121 hours (SAL at 8,000 training seeds) to as much as 3,308 hours (SPL at 2,000 training seeds).

So How Much Can I Save with CAL?

"A lot" is the answer, based on the Grossman/Cormack research. We have published similar studies with similar results. Given this evidence, it is hard to imagine why anyone would use these out-of-date TAR protocols.

There are a number of other benefits that go beyond cost and time savings. First, CAL works well with low richness collections, as Grossman/Cormack point out. While some populations have high percentages of relevant documents, not all do. Why not choose one protocol that covers both ends of the spectrum equally well?

Second, as mentioned earlier, the CAL protocol allows for the continuous addition of documents without need for costly and time-consuming retraining. Simply add the new documents to the collection and keep reviewing. This is particularly true if you use our contextual diversity engine to find documents that are different from those you have already seen. Contextual diversity protects against the possibility of bias stemming from using documents found through keyword searches.

Third, review can begin right away. With TAR 1.0 protocols, the review team can't begin until an SME does the training. Depending on the SME's inclination to look at random documents and schedule, the review can be help up for days or weeks. With CAL, the review starts right away.

These are just a few ways in which the TAR 1.0 protocols cause real world problems. Why pay more in review costs and time to use an inferior protocol? How much can you save with CAL?

4

Continuous Active Learning for Technology Assisted Review

How It Works and Why It Matters for E-Discovery

Two of the leading experts on e-discovery, Maura R. Grossman and Gordon V. Cormack, presented a peer-reviewed study on continuous active learning to the annual conference of the Special Interest Group on Information Retrieval, a part of the Association for Computing Machinery (ACM), "Evaluation of Machine-Learning Protocols for Technology-Assisted Review in Electronic Discovery."

In the study, they compared three TAR protocols, testing them across eight different cases. Two of the three protocols, Simple Passive Learning (SPL) and Simple Active Learning (SAL), are typically associated with early approaches to predictive coding, which we call TAR 1.0. The third, continuous active learning (CAL), is a central part of a newer approach to predictive coding, which we call TAR 2.0.

Based on their testing, Grossman and Cormack concluded that CAL demonstrated superior performance over SPL and SAL, while avoiding certain other problems associated with these traditional TAR 1.0 protocols. Specifically, in each of the eight case studies, CAL reached higher levels of recall (finding relevant documents) more quickly and with less effort that the TAR 1.0 protocols.

Not surprisingly, their research caused quite a stir in the TAR community. Supporters heralded its common-sense findings, particularly the conclusion that random training was the least efficient method for selecting training seeds. (See, e.g., "Latest Grossman and Cormack Study Proves Folly of Using Random Search for Machine Training", by Ralph Losey on his e-Discovery Team blog) Detractors challenged their results, arguing that using random seeds for training worked fine with their TAR 1.0 software and eliminated bias. (See, e.g., "Random Sampling as an Effective Predictive Coding Training Strategy", by Herbert L. Roitblat on OrcaBlog). We were pleased that it confirmed our earlier research and legitimized what for many is still a novel approach to TAR review.

So why does this matter? The answer is simple. CAL matters because saving time and money on review is important to our clients. The more the savings, the more it matters.

TAR 1.0: Predictive Coding Protocols

To better understand how CAL works and why it produces better results, let's start by taking a look at TAR 1.0 protocols and their limitations.

Most are built around the following steps:

1. A subject matter expert (SME), often a senior lawyer, reviews and tags a random sample (500+ documents) to use as a control set for training.

2. The SME then begins a training process using Simple Passive Learning or Simple Active Learning. In either case, the SME reviews documents and tags them relevant or non-relevant.

3. The TAR engine uses these judgments to train a classification/ ranking algorithm to identify other relevant documents. It compares its results against the already-tagged control set to gauge its accuracy in identifying relevant documents.

4. Depending on the testing results, the SME may need to do more training to improve performance of a particular classification/ ranking project (often referred to as a "classifier").

5. This training and testing process continues until the classifier is "stable." That means its search algorithm is no longer getting better at identifying relevant documents in the control set. There is no point in further training relative to the control set.

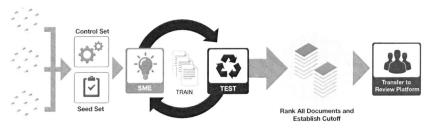

The next step is for the TAR engine to run its classification/ranking algorithm against the entire document population. The SME can then review a random sample of ranked documents to determine how well the algorithm did in pushing relevant documents to the top of the ranking. The sample will help tell the review administrator how many documents will need to be reviewed to reach different recall rates.

The review team can then be directed to look at documents with relevance scores higher than the cutoff point. Documents below the cutoff point can be discarded.

Even though training is initially iterative, it is a finite process. Once your classifier has learned all it can about the 500+ documents in the control set, that's it. You simply turn it loose to rank the larger population (which can take hours to complete) and then divide the documents into categories to review or not review.

The goal, to be sure, is for the review population to be smaller than the remainder. Savings come from not having to review all of the documents.

SPL and SAL: Simple TAR 1.0 Training Protocols

Grossman and Cormack tested two training protocols used in the TAR 1.0 methodology: Simple Passive Learning and Simple Active Learning.

Simple Passive Learning uses random documents for training. Grossman and Cormack did not find this approach to be particularly effective:

> *The results show that entirely non-random training methods, in which the initial training documents are selected using a simple keyword search, and subsequent training documents are selected by active learning, require substantially and significantly less human review effort to achieve any given level of recall, than passive learning, in which the machine-learning algorithm plays no role in the selection of training documents.*

Common sense supports their conclusion. The quicker you can present relevant documents to the system, the faster it should learn about your documents.

Simple Active Learning does not rely on random documents. Instead, it suggests starting with whatever relevant documents you can find, often through keyword search, to initiate the training. From there, the computer presents additional documents designed to help train the algorithm. Typically the system selects documents it is least sure about, often from the boundary between relevance and non-relevance. In effect, the machine learning algorithm is trying to figure out where to draw the line between the two based on the documents in the control set you created to start the process.

As Grossman and Cormack point out, this means that the SME spends a lot of time looking at marginal documents in order to train the classifier. And keep in mind that the classifier is training against a relatively small number of documents chosen by your initial random sample. There is no statistical reason to think these are in fact representative of the larger population and likely are not.

Grossman and Cormack concluded that Simple Active Learning performed better than Simple Passive Learning. However, Simple Active Learning was found to be less effective than continuous active learning.

Among active-learning methods, continuous active learning with relevance feedback yields generally superior results to simple active learning with uncertainty sampling, while avoiding the vexing issue of "stabilization"—determining when training is adequate, and therefore may stop.

Thus, both of the TAR 1.0 protocols, SPL and SAL, were found to be less effective at finding relevant documents than CAL.

Practical Problems with TAR 1.0 Protocols

Whether you use either the SPL or SAL protocol, the TAR 1.0 process comes with a number of practical problems when applied to "real world" discovery.

One Bite at the Apple: The first, and most relevant to a discussion of continuous active learning, is that you get only "one bite at the apple." Once the team gets going on the review set, there is no opportunity to feed back their judgments on review documents and improve the classification/ranking algorithm. Improving the algorithm means the review team will have to review less documents to reach any desired recall level.

SMEs Required: A second problem is that TAR 1.0 generally requires a senior lawyer or subject-matter expert (SME) for training. Expert training requires the lawyer to review thousands of documents to build a control set, to train and then test the results. Not only is this expensive, but it delays the review until you can convince your busy senior attorney to sit still and get through the training.

Rolling Uploads: Going further, the TAR 1.0 approach does not handle rolling uploads well and does not work well for low richness collections, both of which are common in e-discovery. New documents render the control set invalid because they were not part of the random selection process. That typically means going through new training rounds.

Low Richness: The problem with low richness collections is that it can be hard to find good training examples based on random sampling. If richness is below 1%, you may have to review several thousand documents just to find enough relevant ones to train the system. Indeed, this issue is sufficiently difficult that some TAR 1.0 vendors suggest their products shouldn't be used for low richness collections.

TAR 2.0: Continuous Active Learning Protocols

With TAR 2.0, these real-world problems go away, partly due to the nature of continuous learning and partly due to the continuous ranking process required to support continuous learning. Taken together, continuous learning and continuous ranking form the basis of the TAR 2.0 approach, not only saving on review time and costs but making the process more fluid and flexible in the bargain.

Continuous Ranking

Our TAR 2.0 engine is designed to rank millions of documents in minutes. As a result, we rank every document in the collection each time we run a ranking. That means we can continuously integrate new judgments by the review team into the algorithm as their work progresses.

Because the engine ranks all of the documents all of the time, there is no need to use a control set for training. Training success is based on ranking fluctuations across the entire set, rather than a limited set of randomly selected documents. When document rankings stop changing, the classification/ranking algorithm has settled, at least until new documents arrive.

This solves the problem of rolling uploads. Because we don't use a control set for training, we can integrate rolling document uploads into the review process. When you add new documents to the mix, they simply join in the ranking process and become part of the review.

Depending on whether the new documents are different or similar to documents already in the population, they may integrate into the rankings immediately or instead fall to the bottom. In the latter case, we pull samples from the new documents through our contextual diversity algorithm for review. As the new documents are reviewed, they integrate further into the ranking.

You can see an illustration of the initial fluctuation of new documents in this example from Insight Predict. The initial review moved forward until the classification/ranking algorithm was pretty well trained.

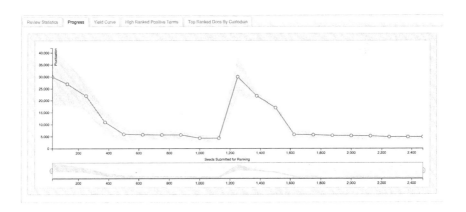

New documents were added to the collection midway through the review process. Initially the population rankings fluctuated to accommodate the new documents. Then, as representative samples were identified and reviewed, the population settled down to stability.

Continuous Active Learning

There are two aspects to continuous active learning. The first is that the process is "continuous." Training doesn't stop until the review finishes. The second is that the training is "active." That means the computer feeds documents to the review team with the goal of making the review as efficient as possible (minimizing the total cost of review).

Although our software will support a TAR 1.0 process, we have long advocated continuous active learning as the better protocol. Simply put, as the reviewers progress through documents in our system, we feed their judgments back to the system to be used as seeds in the next ranking process. Then, when the reviewers ask for a new batch, the documents are presented based on the latest completed ranking. To the extent the ranking has improved by virtue of the additional review judgments, they receive better documents than they otherwise would had the learning stopped after "one bite at the apple."

In effect, the reviewers become the trainers and the trainers becom reviewers. Training is review, we say. And review is training.

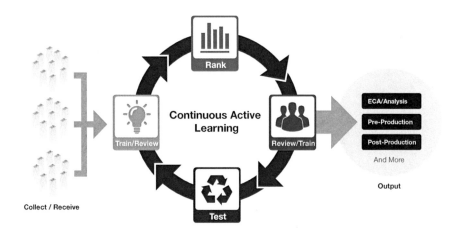

Indeed, review team training is all but required for a continuous learning process. It makes little sense to expect a senior attorney do the entire review, which may involve hundreds of thousands of documents. Rather, SMEs should focus on finding (through search or otherwise) relevant documents to help move the training forward as quickly as possible. They can also be used to monitor the review team, using our quality control ("QC") algorithm designed to surface documents likely to have been improperly tagged. We have shown that this process is as effective as using senior lawyers to do the training and can be done at a lower cost. And, like CAL itself, our QC algorithm also continues to learn as the review progresses.

What are the Savings?

Grossman and Cormack quantified the differences between the TAR 1.0 and 2.0 protocols by measuring the number of documents a team would need to review to get to a specific recall rate. Here, for example, is a chart showing the difference in the number of documents a team would have to review to achieve a 75% level of recall comparing continuous active learning and simple passive learning.

Review Effort to Achieve 75% Recall

Matter	CAL Total Effort	SPL Training Phase Effort	SPL Review Phase Effort	SPL Total Effort
201	6,000	44,000	12,000	56,000
202	11,000	7,000	19,000	26,000
203	6,000	9,000	90,000	99,000
207	11,000	9,000	26,000	35,000
A	11,000	27,000	58,000	85,000
B	8,000	7,000	13,000	20,000
C	4,000	3,000	4,000	7,000
D	18,000	6,000	31,000	37,000

Total Effort is measured in terms of the number of documents reviewed to achieve the target recall of 75%. For CAL, Total Effort includes both training and review, which are not separate phases. For SPL, training and review are distinct phases; thus, Total Effort reflects the sum of both.

The test results showed that the review team would have to look at substantially more documents using the SPL (random seeds) protocol than CAL. For matter 201, the difference would be 50,000 documents. At $2 a document for review and QC, that would be a savings of $100,000. For matter 203, which is the extreme case here, the difference would be 93,000 documents. The savings from using CAL based on $2 a document would be $186,000.

Here is another chart that compares all three protocols over the same test set. In this case Grossman and Cormack varied the size of the training sets for SAL and SPL to see what impact it might have on the review numbers. You can see that the results for both of the TAR 1.0 protocols improve with additional training but at the cost of requiring the SME to look at as many as 8,000 documents before beginning training. And, even using what Grossman and Cormack call an "ideal" training set for SAL and SPL (which cannot be identified in advance), SAL beat or matched the results in every case, often by a substantial margin.

Matter	CAL	SAL 2K	SAL 5K	SAL 8K	SAL Ideal	SPL 2K	SPL 5K	SPL 8K	SPL Ideal
201	6	237	7	10	7	284	331	164	56
202	11	34	12	14	12	47	29	26	26
203	6	43	7	10	6	521	331	154	99
207	11	55	23	13	13	103	50	36	35
A	11	210	42	12	12	502	326	204	85
B	8	119	10	11	10	142	41	21	20
C	4	5	8	10	5	9	8	10	7
D	18	60	54	53	18	55	38	37	37

What About Review Bias?

Grossman and Cormack constructed their CAL protocol by starting with seeds found through keyword search. They then presented documents to reviewers based on "relevance feedback."

Relevance feedback simply means that the system feeds the highest-ranked documents to the reviewers for their judgment. Of course, what is highly ranked depends on what you tagged before.

Some argue that this approach opens the door to bias. If your ranking is based on documents you found through keyword search, what about other relevant documents you didn't find? "You don't know what you don't know," they say.

Random selection of training seeds raises the chance of finding relevant documents that are different from the ones you have already found. Right?

Actually, everyone seems to agree on this point. Grossman and Cormack point out that they used relevance feedback because they wanted to keep their testing methods simple and reproducible. As they note in their conclusion:

> There is no reason to presume that the CAL results described here represent the best that can be achieved. Any number of feature engineering methods, learning algorithms, training protocols, and search strategies might yield substantive improvements in the future.

In an excellent four-part series on his blog e-Discovery Team, RalphLosey suggested using a multi-modal approach to combat fears of bias in the training process. From private discussions with the authors, we know that Grossman and Cormack also use added techniques to improve the learning process for their system as well.

We combat bias in our active learning process by including contextual diversity samples as part of our active training protocol. Contextual diversity uses an algorithm we developed to present the reviewer with documents that are very different from what the review team has already seen. We wrote about it extensively in a recent blog post.

Our ability to do contextual diversity sampling comes from the fact that our engine ranks all of the documents every time. Because we rank all the documents, we know something about the nature of the documents already seen by the reviewers and the documents not yet reviewed. The contextual diversity algorithm essentially clusters unseen documents and then presents a representative sample of each group as the review progresses. And, like our relevance and QC algorithms, contextual diversity also keeps learning and improving as the review progresses.

The Continuous Learning Process

Backed by our continuous ranking engine and contextual diversity, we can support a simple and flexible TAR 2.0 process for training and review. Here are the basic steps:

1. Start by finding as many relevant documents as possible. Feed them to the system for initial ranking. (Actually, you could start with no relevant documents and build off of the review team's work. Or, start with contextual diversity sampling to get a feel for different types of documents in the population.)

2. Let the review team begin review. They get an automated mix including highly relevant documents and others selected by the computer based on contextual diversity and randomness to avoid bias. Our mix is a trade secret but most are highly ranked documents to maximize review-team efficiency over the course of the entire review.

3. As the review progresses, QC a small percentage of the documents at the senior attorney's leisure. Our QC algorithm will present documents that are most likely tagged incorrectly.

4. Continue until you reach the desired recall rate. Track your progress through our progress chart (shown above) and an occasional systematic sample, which will generate a yield curve.

The process is flexible and can progress in almost any way you desire You can start with tens of thousands of tagged documents if you have them, or start with just a few or none at all. Just let the review team get going either way and let the system balance the mix of documents included in the dynamic, continuously iterative review queue. As they finish batches, the ranking engine keeps getting smarter. If you later find relevant documents through whatever means, simply add them. It just doesn't matter when your goal is to find relevant documents for review rather than train a classifier.

This TAR 2.0 process works well with low richness collections because you are encouraged to start the training with any relevant documents you can find. As review progresses, more relevant documents rise to the top of the rankings, which means your trial team can get up to speed more quickly. It also works well for ECA and third-party productions where you need to get up to speed quickly.

Key Differences Between TAR 1.0 and 2.0

TAR 1.0	TAR 2.0
1. One Time Training before assigning documents for review. Does not allow for training or learning past the initial training phase.	**1. Continuous Active Learning** allows the algorithm to keep improving over the course of review, improving savings and speed.
2. Trains Against Small Reference Set, limiting its ability to handle rolling uploads. Assumes all documents are received before ranking. Stability is based on comparison with reference set.	**2. Analyzes and Ranks Entire Collection Every Time**, which allows rolling uploads. Does not use a reference set, but rather evaluates performance using multiple measures across the entire population.
3. Subject Matter Expert handles all training. Review team judgments are not used to further train the system.	**3. Review Teams Train** as they review, working alongside SME for maximum effectiveness. SME can focus on finding relevant documents and performing QC on review team judgments.
4. Uses Random Seeds to train the system and avoid bias, precluding or limiting the use of key documents found by the trial team.	**4. Uses Judgmental Seeds** so that training can immediately use every relevant document available. Supplements training with active learning to avoid bias.
5. Doesn't Work Well with low richness collections, where target documents are rare. Impractical for smaller cases because of stilted workflow.	**5. Works Great** in low richness situations. Ideal for any size case from small to huge because of flexible workflow with no separate, burdensome training phases.

Conclusion

As Grossman and Cormack point out:

> This study highlights an alternative approach—continuous active learning with relevance feedback—that demonstrates superior performance, while avoiding certain problems associated with uncertainty sampling and passive learning. CAL also offers the reviewer the opportunity to quickly identify legally significant documents that can guide litigation strategy, and can readily adapt when new documents are added to the collection, or new issues or interpretations of relevance arise.

If your TAR product is integrated into your review engine and supports continuous ranking, there is little doubt they are right. Keep learning, get smarter and save more. That is a winning combination.

Introduction to TAR: Chapter 5

5

Five Questions to Ask Your E-Discovery Vendor About Continuous Active Learning

In the aftermath of recent studies showing that continuous active learning (CAL) is more effective than the first-generation TAR 1.0 protocols, it seems like every e-discovery vendor is jumping on the bandwagon. At the least it feels like every e-discovery vendor claims to use CAL or somehow incorporate it into their TAR protocols.

Despite these claims, there remains a wide chasm between the TAR protocols available on the market today. As a TAR consumer, how can you determine whether a vendor that claims to use CAL actually does? Below are five basic questions you can ask your vendor to ensure that your review effectively employs CAL.

1. Does Your TAR Tool Use a Control Set for Training?

Control sets are the hallmark of TAR 1.0, but wholly inconsistent with the concept of CAL. In fact, the use of a control set for training can often impair and complicate the TAR process.

To train a TAR 1.0 tool, you typically start by generating a random sample to represent the entire document population to some statistical degree of certainty. That random sample—a small fraction of the entire collection—is considered the control set. As documents are reviewed and coded, the progress of training is measured against the control set, which is re-ranked after every training round. Once it appears that training is having little impact on the ranking of the control set, the tool is considered to be stabilized. The one-time training effort concludes and the tool is used to rank the entire collection for production review.

By comparison, a true CAL process uses no control set. Every review decision is used to train the tool, and the entire collection (not a small subset) is constantly re-ranked and monitored. Only when it appears that you have reached your goal vis-a-vis the entire collection, or that training is having no further impact on the ranking of the entire collection and responsive documents are no longer being returned for review, do review and training cease.

2. Does Training Focus on Marginally Relevant Documents or Highly Relevant Documents?

Training that focuses on marginally relevant documents will not optimize the use of CAL. In fact, TAR protocols that focus on marginally relevant documents are typically not CAL and are generally less effective.

The predominant objective of reviewing marginally relevant documents is to determine where best to draw the line between relevant and non-relevant documents. The ultimate goal is to train an algorithm, called a "classifier," to make that distinction, so the presumptively relevant documents can be separately reviewed for production. Generally, TAR protocols that use a classifier to segregate documents neither rank the collection nor train continuously through the attainment of review objectives. Thus, they would not be considered CAL.

As illustrated by the below chart, the classifier approach has two drawbacks. First, no matter how well the line is drawn, some number of relevant documents (either cats or dogs) will fall on the other side of the line and never be seen in the review set. Second, the tighter you try to draw that line, the more time and effort it takes before you can even begin to review documents.

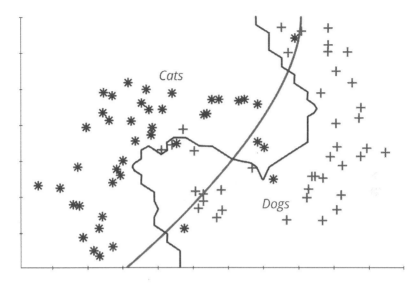

Conversely, the objective of CAL is to continuously use reviewer judgments to improve training and rank the collection, and to use the improved ranking to present the reviewers with better documents. This process continues iteratively until the review targets are achieved for the collection as a whole. To implement this protocol effectively, training and review focus primarily and specifically on highly relevant documents. There is no wasted effort, and every relevant document is available for review.

3. How Often Do You Rank the Collection During Review?

The essence of CAL is its ability to harness reviewer judgments to rank the collection and return the best documents to the reviewers as early as possible. Every time CAL ranks the collection, reviewer judgments are leveraged to improve review and, in turn, to improve the next ranking. The process is cyclical and the results exponential.

Studies prove the obvious—the more frequent the ranking, the better the results. This phenomenon is akin to compounding interest. The more frequently interest is compounded, the more rapidly the benefit accrues. With CAL, the more frequently the collection is ranked, the more rapidly reviewers can take advantage of their collective decisions to successively feed judgments back to the tool for further refinement.

Among vendors, a tremendous disparity exists in the frequency with which they rank the collection (or the control set, with TAR 1.0). Catalyst, for example, can and does rank millions of documents in minutes. Reviewer judgments are used to rank the entire collection several times every hour throughout the review and training process. Most other vendors rank only the control set (not the collection) during review and training, and subsequently rank the entire collection only once. Even worse, their process of ranking the entire collection can typically take several hours to complete.

4. Is It Necessary to Have a Subject Matter Expert do the Training?

Although TAR 1.0 requires a subject matter expert (SME) for training, CAL does not. In fact, since all review is training with CAL, training by an SME would be prohibitive. CAL frees the SME to focus on more productive tasks and leave the bulk training to the reviewers. This enables immediate review and eliminates the time and expense associated with training a TAR 1.0 tool.

With TAR 1.0, training is a one-time effort, the results are driven by comparison to a finite control set, and the process dictates exactly which documents will be reviewed for production. This creates an inherent need for the consistency of a single decision maker with the knowledge and authority to establish the scope of the eventual review.

This is not the case with CAL, where every review judgment trains the tool. Reviewers see the same documents they would have seen after training using a TAR 1.0 protocol (perhaps more), and presumably make the same decisions. Because the tool is continuously learning from the reviewers' judgments, the universe of documents passed to the reviewers is constantly refined to elevate those most likely to be produced.

The upshot of eliminating SME review is savings—of both time and money. TAR 1.0 typically requires at least two weeks of SME effort before the review team can review a single document. Given the billing rate of senior attorneys most likely to serve as SMEs, that effort will cost tens of thousands of dollars. With CAL, review and training are coextensive and start immediately, with no sunk cost for training.

5. What is Your Process for Handling Rolling Collections?

The reality of modern discovery is that all of the documents to be reviewed for production are rarely available at the same time. Instead, documents are collected piecemeal and arrive on a rolling basis. An added benefit of CAL is its ability to incorporate new documents into the collection at virtually any point in the review without sacrificing previous effort. If the vendor suggests that a rolling collection presents any impediment to seamless review, the vendor is not making an efficient or effective use of CAL.

Rolling collections are a problem for TAR 1.0 protocols because they rely on control sets for training. A control set is intended to represent the entire collection. Since newly added documents change the character of the collection, the initial control set is no longer representative. Every time documents are added to a collection, a new, revised or additional control set needs to be generated. Even worse, if new documents are added after training is completed and a review set generated, it may be necessary to completely retrain the tool in addition to preparing a new control set.

CAL is not subject to these limitations. As new documents are received, they are simply incorporated into the collection and integrated according to the current ranking. As those documents are reviewed and coded through the continuous-learning process, the ranking adjusts to reflect the new information. No effort is lost. Every previous judgment remains intact and every subsequent judgment further improves the ranking.

Bonus Question: How Easy Is It to Run Simultaneous TAR Projects?

Another benefit of CAL is the ability to run simultaneous TAR projects and generate useful results almost immediately, at any point during the review and with little to no additional setup. With TAR 1.0, the process is much more cumbersome. If your vendor does not allow you to easily and quickly implement simultaneous TAR projects, you are not using CAL to its fullest potential.

Since review is training with CAL, very little is required to run simultaneous TAR projects covering different issues. Simply identify each of the pertinent issues and code the documents for each issue during review. The tool will use each judgment, and generate and maintain a separate ranking for each issue. Once you attain the review objective for one TAR project, you can focus on the next project. The existing ranking will make every successive project more efficient.

CAL can incorporate new TAR projects at any point during review and quickly generate results. Review and coding for a new project can start as soon as a new issue is identified. From that point forward, every review decision can include a judgment on the new issue. By focusing specifically on the new TAR project, review and training will quickly improve the ranking and return the best documents for further review.

TAR 1.0 is too cumbersome to do this effectively. With TAR 1.0, every project requires a separately coded control set against which to evaluate training. This makes simultaneous projects, especially new projects arising during review, difficult to implement.

CAL provides significant advantages over other TAR protocols, in both efficiency and effectiveness. So how can you be sure that your vendor is actually equipping your review project with all of the benefits of an efficient and effective CAL protocol? Just ask five simple questions— and throw in the bonus for good measure.

6

TAR 2.0 Capabilities Allow Use in Even More E-Discovery Tasks

Recent advances in technology sssisted review ("TAR 2.0") include the ability to deal with low richness, rolling collections, and flexible inputs in addition to vast improvements in speed. These improvements now allow TAR to be used effectively in many more discovery workflows than its traditional "TAR 1.0" use in classifying large numbers of documents for production.

To better understand this, it helps to begin by examining in more detail the kinds of tasks we face. Broadly speaking, document review tasks fall into three categories:

- **Classification**. This is the most common form of document review, in which documents are sorted into buckets such as responsive or non-responsive so that we can do something different with each class of document. The most common example here is a review for production.

- **Protection**. This is a higher level of review in which the purpose is to protect certain types of information from disclosure.

The most common example is privilege review, but this also encompasses trade secrets and other forms of confidential, protected, or even embarrassing information, such as personally identifiable information (PII) or confidential supervisory information (CSI).

- **Knowledge Generation**. The goal here is learning what stories the documents can tell us and discovering information that could prove useful to our case. A common example of this is searching and reviewing documents received in a production from an opposing party or searching a collection for documents related to specific issues or deposition witnesses.

You're probably already quite familiar with these types of tasks, but I want to get explicit and discuss them in detail because each of the three has distinctly different recall and precision targets, which in turn have important implications for designing your workflows and integrating TAR.

Metrics

Let's quickly review those two crucial metrics for measuring the effectiveness and defensibility of your discovery processes, "recall" and "precision." Recall is a measure of completeness, the percentage of relevant documents actually retrieved. Precision measures purity, the percentage of retrieved documents that are relevant.

The higher the percentage of each, the better you've done. If you achieve 100% recall, then you have retrieved all the relevant documents. If all the documents you retrieve are relevant and have no extra junk mixed in, you've achieved 100% precision. But recall and precision are not friends. Typically, a technique that increases one will decrease the other.

This engineering trade-off between recall and precision is why it helps to be explicit and think carefully about what we're trying to accomplish. Because the three categories of document review have different recall and precision targets, we must choose and tune our technologies—including TAR—with these specific goals in mind so that we maximize effectiveness and minimize cost and risk. Let me explain in more detail.

Classification Tasks

Start with classification—the sorting of documents into buckets. We typically classify so that we can do different things with different subpopulations, such as review, discard, or produce.

Under the Federal Rules of Civil Procedure, and as emphasized by The Sedona Conference and any number of court opinions, e-discovery is limited by principles of reasonableness and proportionality. As Magistrate Judge Andrew J. Peck wrote in the seminal case, *Da Silva Moore v. Publicis Groupe*:

> *The goal is for the review method to result in higher recall and higher precision than another review method, at a cost proportionate to the value of the case.*

As Judge Peck suggests, when we're talking document production the goal is to get better results, not perfect results. Given this, you want to achieve reasonably high percentages of recall and precision, but with cost and effort that is proportionate to the case. Thus, a goal of 80% recall—a common TAR target—could well be reasonable when reviewing for responsive documents, especially when current research suggests that the "gold standard" of complete eyes-on review by attorneys can't do any better than that at many times the cost.[1]

Precision must also be reasonable, but requesting parties are usually more interested in making sure they get as many responsive documents as possible. So recall usually gets more attention here.[2]

Protection Tasks

By contrast, when your task is to protect certain types of confidential information (most commonly privilege, but it could be trade secrets, confidential supervisory information, or anything else where the bell can't be unrung), you need to achieve 100% recall. Period. Nothing can fall through the cracks. This tends to be problematic in practice, as the goal is absolute perfection and the real world seldom obliges.

So to approximate this perfection in practice, we usually need to use every tool in our toolkit to identify the documents that need to be protected—not just TAR but also keyword searching and human review—and use them effectively against each other. The reason for this is simple: Different review methods make different kinds of mistakes. Human reviewers tend to make random mistakes. TAR systems tend to make very systematic errors, getting entire classifications of documents right or wrong.[3] By combining different techniques into our workflows, one serves as a check against the others.

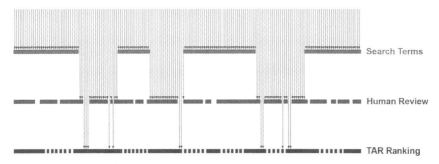

The best way to maximize recall is to stack techniques.

This is an important point about TAR for data protection tasks, and one I want to reemphasize. The best way to maximize recall is to stack techniques, not to replace them. Because TAR doesn't make the same class of errors as search terms and human review, it makes an excellent addition to privilege and other data protection workflows— provided the technology can deal with low prevalence and be efficiently deployed.[4]

Precision, on the other hand, is somewhat less important when your task is to protect documents. Precision doesn't need to be perfect, but because these tasks typically use lots of attorney hours, they're usually the most expensive part of review. Including unnecessary junk gets expensive quickly. So you still want to achieve a fairly high level of precision (particularly to avoid having to log documents unnecessarily if you are maintaining a privilege log), but recall is still the key metric here.

Knowledge Generation Tasks

The final task we described is where we get the name "discovery" in the first place. What stories do these documents tell? What stories can my opponents tell with these documents? What facts and knowledge can we learn from them? This is the discovery task that is most Google-like.[5] For knowledge generation, we don't really care about recall. We don't want all the documents about a topic; we just want the best documents about a topic—the ones that will end up in front of deponents or used at trial.

Precision is therefore the most important metric here. You don't want to waste your time going through junk—or even duplicative and less relevant documents. This is where TAR can also help, prioritizing the document population by issue and concentrating the most interesting documents at the top of the list so that attorneys can quickly learn what they need to litigate the case.

One nitpicky detail about TAR for issue coding and knowledge generation should be mentioned, though. TAR algorithms rank documents according to their likelihood of getting a thumbs-up or a thumbs-down from a human reviewer. They do not rank documents based on how interesting they are. For example, in a review for responsiveness, some documents could be very easy to predict as being responsive, but not very interesting. On the other hand, some documents could be extremely interesting, but harder to predict because they are so unusual.

On the gripping hand, however, the more interesting documents tend to cluster near the top of the ranking. Interesting documents sort higher this way because they tend to contain stronger terms and concepts as well as more of them.[6] TAR's ability to concentrate the interesting documents near the top of a ranked list thus makes it a useful addition to knowledge-generation workflows.

What's Next

With this framework for thinking about, developing, and evaluating different discovery workflows, we can now get into the specifics of how TAR 2.0 can best be used for the various tasks at hand. To help with this analysis, we have created a TAR checklist (http://www.catalystsecure.com/TARchecklist) you can use to help organize your approach.

In the end, the critical factor in your success will be how effectively you use all the tools and resources you have at your disposal, and TAR 2.0 is a powerful new addition to your toolbox.

Footnotes

1. See, e.g., Maura R. Grossman & Gordon V. Cormack, *Technology-Assisted Review in E-Discovery Can Be More Effective and More Efficient Than Exhaustive Manual Review*, XVII RICH. J.L. & TECH. 11 (2011), at 10-15 (summarizing recent research on human review and citing results for maxima of 65% recall (*Voorhees* 2000) and 52.8% – 83.6% recall (*Roitblat, Kershaw, & Oot* 2010)).

2. The differing importance of recall and precision both here and in other discovery tasks is one reason the F_1 measure (the harmonic mean of recall and precision) is often problematic. While it may be a good single measure for information retrieval research, it prematurely blends two measures that often have to be considered and weighted separately in practical discovery tasks.

3. See, e.g. Maura R. Grossman and Gordon V. Cormack, *Inconsistent Responsiveness Determination in Document Review: Difference of Opinion or Human Error?*, 32 Pace L. Rev. 267 (2012), (finding that coding inconsistencies by human reviewers are largely attributable to human error, and not to documents being "borderline" or any inherent ambiguity in the relevance judgments).

4. Random training approaches such as those used by support vector machine algorithms tend to need prohibitively large samples in order to deal effectively with low richness, which is common in many actual cases. See, e.g. Gordon V. Cormack and Maura R. Grossman, *Evaluation of Machine-*

Learning Protocols for Technology-Assisted Review in Electronic Discovery, SIGIR '14, July 6–11, 2014, Gold Coast, Queensland, Australia (evaluating different approaches to TAR training across eight data sets with prevalence (richness) ranging from 0.25% to 3.92% with a mean of 1.18%).

5. To be more nitpicky, this search is the most Google-like for the basic task of searching on a single topic. A more challenging problem here is often figuring out all the different possible topic that a collection of documents could speak to—including those that we don't know we need to look for— and then finding the best examples of each topic to review. This is another area where TAR and similar tools that model the entire document set can be useful.

6. This is true in general, but not always. Consider an email between two key custodians who are usually chatty but that reads simply "Call me." There are no key terms there for a ranking engine based on full text analysis to latch onto, though the unusual email could be susceptible to other forms of outlier detection and search.

7

Measuring Recall for E-Discovery Review

An Introduction to Recall Sampling

A critical metric in technology assisted review (TAR) is recall, which is the percentage of relevant documents actually found from the collection. One of the most compelling reasons for using TAR is the promise that a review team can achieve a desired level of recall (say 75%) after reviewing only a small portion of the total document population (say 5%). The savings come from not having to review the remaining 95% of the documents. The argument is that the remaining documents (the "discard pile") include so few that are relevant (against so many irrelevant documents) that further review is not economically justified.

How do we prove we have found a given percentage of the relevant documents at whatever point we stop the review? Some suggest you can prove recall by sampling only a relatively few documents, which is not statistically valid. Others suggest approaches that are more statistically valid, but require sampling a lot of documents (as many as 34,000 in one case). Either way, this presents a problem. Legal professionals need a reasonable but also statistically reliable way to measure recall in order to justify review cutoff decisions.

A Hypothetical Review

To illustrate the problem, let's conjure up a hypothetical review. Assume we collected one million documents. Assume also that the percentage of relevant documents in the collection is 1%. That suggests there are 10,000 relevant documents in our collection (1,000,000*.01).

Using Sampling to Estimate Richness

Typically we don't know in advance how many relevant documents are in the collection. To find this information, we need to estimate the collection's richness (aka prevalence) using statistical sampling, which is simply a method in which a sample of the document population is drawn at random, such that statistical properties of the sample may be extrapolated to the entire document population.

To create our sample we must randomly select a subset of the population and use the results to estimate the characteristics of the larger population. The degree of certainty around our estimate is a function of the number of documents we sample.

While this is not meant to be a chapter about statistical sampling, here are a few concepts you should know. Although there are many reference sources for these terms, I will draw from from the excellent, "The Grossman-Cormack Glossary of Technology Assisted Review", 7 Fed. Cts. L. Rev. 1 (2013).:

1. **Point Estimate:** The most likely value for a population characteristic. Thus, when we estimate that a document population contains 10,000 relevant documents, we are offering a point estimate.

2. **Confidence Interval:** A range of values around our point estimate that we believe contains the true value of the number being estimated. For example, if the confidence interval for our point estimate ranges from 8,000 to 12,000, that means we believe the true value will appear within that range.

3. **Margin of Error:** The maximum amount by which a point estimate might deviate from the true value, typically expressed as

percentage. People often talk about a 5% margin of error, which simply means the expected confidence interval is 5% above or below the point estimate.

4. **Confidence Level:** The chance that our confidence interval will include the true value. For example, "95% confidence" means that if one were to draw 100 independent random samples of the same size, and compute the point estimate and confidence interval from each sample, about 95 of the 100 confidence intervals would contain the true value.

5. **Sample Size:** The number of documents we have to sample in order to achieve a specific confidence interval and confidence level. In general, the higher the confidence level, the more documents we have to review. Likewise, if we want a narrower confidence interval, we will have to increase our sample size.

It might help to see these concepts displayed visually. Here is a chart showing what a 95% confidence level looks like against a "normal" distribution of document values as well as a specific confidence interval.

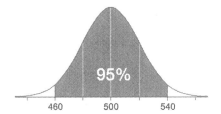

Point Estimate and Confidence Interval

In this case, our point estimate was 500 relevant documents in our collection. Our confidence interval (shaded) suggests that the actual range of relevant documents could go from 460 at the lower end of our estimate to 540 at the higher end.

Part of the curve is not shaded. It covers the 5% chance that the actual number of relevant documents is either above (2.5%) or below (2.5%) our confidence interval range.

Our Hypothetical Estimate

We start our analysis with a sample of 600 documents, chosen randomly from the larger population. The sample size was based on a desired confidence level of 95% and a desired margin of error of 4%. You can use other numbers for this part of the exercise but these will do for our calculations.

How did we get 600? There are a number of online calculators you can use to determine sample size based on your choices about confidence levels and margin of error. We recommend the Raosoft calculator because it is simple to use.

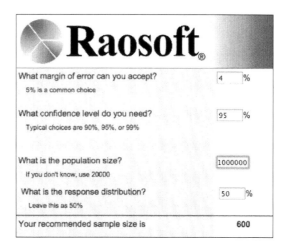

As you can see, we entered the population size (1,000,000), a desired confidence level (95%), and a margin of error (4%). In turn, the calculator suggested that we look at 600 documents for our sample.

Initial Sampling Results

Let's assume we found six relevant documents out of the 600 we sampled. That translates to 0.01 or 1% richness (6/600). We can use that percentage to estimate that there are 10,000 relevant documents in the total review population (1,000,000*.01). This becomes our point estimate.

What about the margin of error? In this case we chose a sample size that would give us up to a 4% margin of error. That means the estimated number of relevant documents in our population is within a 4% range +/- of our point estimate of 10,000 documents.

As noted, there are a million documents in the collection. Four percent of one million comes to 40,000 documents. If we use that figure for our margin of error, it suggests that our confidence interval for relevant documents could range from the six we found in our sample to as high as 50,000. That is an interesting spread.

Determining the Exact Confidence Interval

In practice we would use a more refined approach to calculate our confidence interval. It turns out that the "exact" confidence interval depends on the results of the random sample. In this case we will use a binomial calculator to incorporate the survey results to determine our exact confidence interval.

Binomial Confidence Intervals

Enter the observed numerator and denominator counts, then click the **Compute** button:

Numerator (x):	6
Denominator (N):	600
Compute	
Proportion (x/N):	0.0100

Exact Confidence Interval around Proportion: 0.0037   to   0.0216

Based on our planned sample size (600) and the number of relevant documents we found (6), our confidence interval (expressed as a decimal) ranges from 0.0037 (lower) to 0.0216 (upper). We multiply these decimal values against the total number of documents in our collection (1,000,000) to calculate our exact confidence interval. In this case, it runs from 3,700 to 21,600.

So, we have a start on the problem. We believe there are 10,000 relevant documents in our collection (our point estimate) but it could be as high as 21,600 (or as low as 3,700). Let's move on to our review.

The Review

The team finds 7,500 relevant documents after looking at the first 50,000. Based on our initial point estimate, we could reasonably conclude we have found 75% of the relevant documents. At that point, we might decide to shut down the review. Most courts would view stopping at 75% recall to be more than reasonable.

Your argument to the court seems compelling. If there were only 2,500 relevant documents left in the discard pile, the cost of reviewing another 950,000 documents to find 2,500 relevant ones seems disproportionate. On average, you would have to look at 380 documents to find the next relevant document. At a cost of $2 per document for review, it would cost $760 for each additional relevant document found. If you continued until the end, the cost would be an extra $1.9 million.

How Do We Know We Achieved 75% Recall?

Now comes the hard part. How do we know we actually found 75% of the relevant documents?

Remember that our initial point estimate was 10,000 documents, which seems to support this position. However, it had a confidence interval which suggested the real number of relevant documents could be as high as 21,600.

That means our recall estimate could be off by quite a bit. Here are the numbers for this simple mathematical exercise:

- We found 7,500 documents during the review.

- If there are only 10,000 relevant documents in the total population, it is easy to conclude we achieved 75% recall (7,500/10,000).

- However, if there were 21,600 relevant documents in the population (the upper range for the confidence interval), we achieved only 35% recall of relevant documents (7,500/21,600).

Those numbers would give grist for an argument that the producing party did not meet its burden to find a reasonable number of relevant documents. While the team may have found and reviewed 75% of the relevant documents, it is also possible that they found and reviewed only 35%. Most would agree that 35% is not enough to meet your duty as a producing party.

Sampling the Discard Pile

So what do we do about this problem? One answer is to sample the discard population to determine its richness (some call this term elusion). If we could show that there were only a limited number of relevant documents in the discard pile, that would help establish our bona fides.

Let's make some further assumptions. We sample the discard pile (950,000 documents), again reviewing 600 documents based on our choice of a 95% confidence level and a 4% nominal confidence interval.

This time we find two relevant documents, which suggests that the number of relevant documents in the discard pile has dropped to about 0.33% (2/600). From there we can estimate that we would find only 3,135 relevant documents in the discard pile (950,000*0.0033). Added to the 7,500 documents we found in review, that makes a total of 10,635 relevant documents in the collection.

Using that figure we calculate that the review team found about 71% of the relevant documents (7,500/10,635). While not quite 75%, this is a still a number that most courts have accepted as reasonable and proportionate.

What About the Confidence Interval?

But how big is our exact confidence interval? Using our binomial calculator, we get this range:

Binomial Confidence Intervals

Enter the observed numerator and denominator counts, then click the **Compute** button:

Numerator (x):	2
Denominator (N):	600
Compute	
Proportion (x/N):	0.0033

Exact Confidence Interval around Proportion: 0.0004 to 0.0120

Applying these figures to our discard pile, we estimate that there could be as many as 11,400 relevant documents left (0.0120*950,000).

If we add the 7,500 documents already found to the upper value of 11,400 documents from our sample, we get a much lower estimate of recall. Specifically, we are producing 7,500 out of what could be as many as 18,900 relevant documents. That comes to a recall rate of 40% (7,500/18,900).

Is that enough? Again, I suspect most readers—and courts—would say no. Producing just two out of five relevant documents in a population would not seem reasonable.

Increasing the Sample Size

What to do? One option is to try to narrow the margin of error (and ultimately the exact confidence interval) with a larger sample. We will narrow the margin of error to 1% and see how that impacts our analysis.

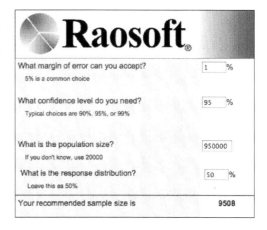

Our calculator suggests we would have to sample 9,508 documents. Assume we find 31 relevant documents out of the 9,508 documents we sampled, which would again support our richness estimate of about 0.33% (31/9508).

We will enter the sampled richness into our binomial calculator to find out our exact confidence interval.

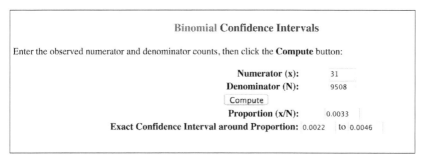

Applying the confidence interval figures to our discard pile we reach the following conclusions:

1. We estimate there are 3,097 relevant documents in the discard pile, about the same as before (950,000*(31/9508)).

2. The lower range of relevant documents is 2,090 (0.0022*950,000).

3. The upper range of relevant documents is 4,370 (0.0046*950,000).

Using these values for our exact confidence interval, the range goes from 63% (7,500/11,870) to 78% (7,500/9,590).

I think most would agree that this type of confidence interval would be reasonable. It would suggest that you found 70% of the relevant documents in your review, with the understanding that the number might be as low as 63% but could be as high as 78%.

The Cost of Proving Recall

We have found a method to prove recall by sampling the discard pile. But at what cost? If we are satisfied with a recall rate of 54% for the lower boundary of our confidence interval, we would have to sample 2,395 documents. At 100 documents an hour, the sample would take about 24 hours of review to complete. At $2 per document, the cost would be $4,790.

If we feel we have to narrow the interval and reach a minimum recall rate of 63%, then the sample size quadruples to 9,508 documents. If we again assume 100 documents an hour, review time would go up to 95 hours, which is more than two weeks of effort. At $2 per document, the cost would jump to $19,016.

To make matters worse, what happens if our confirming sample doesn't support our initial estimate? At that point we would have to continue our review until we found a reasonable percentage. Then we would have to review another sample from the discard pile to confirm that we had indeed found 75% of the relevant documents or whatever number we end up at.

You now see the problem inherent in proving recall. It can require a larger sample size than you might otherwise like.

8

Five Myths About Technology Assisted Review

How TAR 2.0 Overcomes the Limits of Earlier Systems

There was a time when people believed the earth was flat. Or that humans would never walk on the moon. Or that computers had no place in the law. But then the non-believers proved them wrong. The earth is round, men have walked on the moon, and it is hard to imagine practicing law without a computer.

What about technology assisted review? Are there myths surrounding TAR that will fall by the wayside as we better understand the process? Will we look back and smile at what people believed about TAR way back then? Turns out, that is already happening. Here are five myths that early TAR adopters believed true but that modern TAR systems prove wrong.

1. You Only Get One Bite at the Apple.

One early myth about TAR was that you would run it just once and that was the end of it. This myth grew out of the first TAR processes (TAR 1.0), which required an initial seed set of documents selected at random from the total population. A subject matter expert (usually one senior lawyer) tagged each seed document as relevant or irrelevant. The expert's tags were then used to "train" the system. Eventually, after reviewing a few thousand documents, the expert could stop. The system would get no better; it was as well trained about your documents as it could be.

With the training complete, a review administrator applied the TAR algorithm to the rest of the document population. The system ranked the unviewed documents in relevance order. Depending on the effectiveness of the ranking, the administrator set a "cutoff" point to govern the review. Documents ranked higher than the cutoff were reviewed and tagged. Documents below the cutoff were discarded (after confirmatory sampling).

Under this approach, the TAR process was static and run once at the beginning. As reviewers progressed through the documents, there was no easy way to feed their findings back into the system to improve the ranking even further. The myth was that "one bite at the apple" was all you could get.

TAR 2.0 systems let you keep biting away, thanks to their capacity for continuous learning. Now, reviewers are given the next most likely relevant documents for consideration. As they tag the documents (either relevant or not), that information is fed back to the system. As it is, the system gets smarter and smarter about your document population.

The process continues until the review is completed. These TAR 2.0 algorithms continually improve as more review judgments are fed back to the system. The smarter the system gets, the fewer the documents you have to review. The fewer the documents you have to review, the more you save on review time.

2. Subject Matter Experts are Required for TAR Training.

Another myth of TAR 1.0 was that only a subject matter expert can do the training. Although the expert didn't have to be a lawyer, it did have to be someone senior in the field who would know how the documents should be classified. Underlying this myth was the fear that, without an expert, inconsistency in training would degrade the algorithm's effectiveness. That would lead to more documents falling above the cutoff and thus require more expensive human review. Recent evidence suggests this is wrong. First, these senior experts are not always consistent in their tagging. People are fallible. Document review can be mind numbing. On one day, you tag them one way; on another, the opposite.

Second, review teams, while not perfect, turn out to do a pretty good job of tagging documents for training. This is particularly true because most TAR 2.0 systems take this natural variation into account. They can also present outliers to an expert for correction as part of a quality control process. Using reviewers to train the system makes the review cheaper (experts typically bill at higher rates). It also means review can start right away, without the delay of waiting for the busy expert to focus on the review and complete the initial training. Most senior attorneys I know feel they have better things to do than TAR training in any event.

3. You Must Train on Randomly Selected Documents.

Many TAR proponents believe that you need to train the system at least initially using documents selected randomly from the review population. If you select training documents by other means (keyword searching, for example), you may bias the training, they argue. Their fear is that you will unwittingly place undue emphasis on documents you think are relevant while ignoring others that might be equally relevant. "You don't know what you don't know," they say. TAR systems following this approach present the subject matter expert with randomly selected documents for training. This may be tolerable when there are a reasonable number of relevant documents in the population, often called richness. But it can drive you crazy when the population is not rich. You have to click through hundreds if not thousands of documents before you find relevant ones for training.

Modern TAR systems prove this to be a myth. They allow and encourage you to submit as many documents as you can find for training, regardless of how you find them. You supplement this training with documents you don't know about. They can be selected through some form of diversity sampling (specifically, to find documents you know the least about), systematic sampling (sampling every nth document from top to bottom) or even simple random sampling as a supplement but not the main course. The more relevant documents you can find for training, the better the results. Clicking through thousands of random documents is boring and not required for a good TAR result.

4. You Can't Start TAR Training Until You Have All Your Documents.

One of the bugaboos of TAR 1.0 was the requirement that you collect all documents before beginning training. Early systems required this because they trained against a control set rather than against all of the documents. These systems lacked the horsepower to rank all of the documents for each training round. In order for the control set to be valid, it had to be selected randomly from all of the documents being referenced. If you received additional documents the next week, this created a problem. The addition of new documents in the population meant the control set was no longer valid. It was no longer representative of the larger set.

In the real world of litigation, where collections were ongoing, this meant that training had to be redone each time new collections arrived. For review administrators, this represented an impossible burden. They did not have the luxury of waiting until all the documents were collected or of conducting new rounds of training each time new documents were found. TAR 2.0 systems have made this a myth. With the capacity to handle "big data," they rank all of the documents each time and don't use a control set to determine the effectiveness of each ranking.

As a result, new documents can be added continually as they are collected. The new documents may require a few added rounds of training but the process no longer has to start from scratch. They are simply added to the mix and ranked along with the others.

5. TAR Doesn't Work for Non-English Documents.

Many early TAR users believed that the process worked only on English documents. They assumed that TAR systems "understood"the words and concepts in documents. That being the case, there was no way it could understand other languages. This, too, was a myth. TAR is a mathematical process that ranks documents based on word frequency. It has no idea what the words mean. If the documents are prepared properly, TAR can be just as effective with any language as it can with English. For some languages—such as Chinese, Japanese and Korean—this requires that the text is first broken into individual word segments, a process also called tokenizing. Many TAR 1.0 systems did not have tokenizing engines. Many TAR 2.0 systems are able to tokenize. As long as your trainers understand the documents and can tag them properly, TAR should be just as effective with non-English documents as with English ones.

Myths Help Us Understand Our World.

Myths evolved to help us make sense of things that were beyond our comprehension. We created myths about the sun being drawn by chariots or the moon being made of green cheese. Myths helped us get started in understanding our solar system. As we learn more, myths get replaced by facts, which help us to better navigate our world. As we learn more about TAR and the cost-saving benefits it can provide, many of the initial myths about how it worked have fallen away too.

Turns out, the moon is not made of green cheese, nor is the sun drawn by chariots. And TAR is far more versatile and adaptable than early adopters believed.

Reprinted with permission from the January 2014 edition of Law Technology News.

9

Using Continuous Active Learning to Solve the 'Transparency' Issue in Technology Assisted Review

Technology assisted review has a transparency problem. Notwithstanding TAR's proven savings in both time and review costs, many attorneys hesitate to use it because courts require "transparency" in the TAR process.

Specifically, when courts approve requests to use TAR, they often set the condition that counsel disclose the TAR process they used and which documents they used for training. In some cases, the courts have gone so far as to allow opposing counsel to kibitz during the training process itself.

Attorneys fear that this kind of transparency will force them to reveal work product, thoughts about problem documents, or even case strategy. Although most attorneys accept the requirement to share key- word searches as a condition of using them, disclosing their TAR training documents in conjunction with a production seems a step too far.

Thus, instead of using TAR with its concomitant savings, they stick to keyword searches and linear review. For fear of disclosure, the better technology sits idle and its benefits are lost.

The new generation of TAR engines (TAR 2.0), particularly the continuous active learning protocol (CAL), however, enable you to avoid the transparency issue altogether.

Transparency: A TAR 1.0 Problem

Putting aside the issue of whether attorneys are justified in their reluctance, which seems fruitless to debate, consider why this form of transparency is required by the courts.

Limitations of Early TAR. The simple answer is that it arose as an outgrowth of early TAR protocols (TAR 1.0), which used one-time training against a limited set of reference documents (the "control set"). The argument seemed to be that every training call (plus or mi- nus) had a disproportionate impact on the algorithm in that training mistakes could be amplified when the algorithm ran against the full document set. That fear, whether founded or not, led courts to conclude that opposing counsel should be able to oversee the training to ensure costly mistakes weren't made.

Solutions in New TAR. This is not an issue for TAR 2.0, which eschews the one-time training limits of early systems in favor of a continuous active learning protocol (CAL) that continues through to the end of the review. This approach minimizes the impact of reviewer "mistakes" because the rankings are based on tens and sometimes hundreds of thousands of judgments, rather than just a few.

CAL also puts to rest the importance of initial training seeds because training continues throughout the process. The training seeds are in fact all of the relevant documents produced at the end of the process. At most you can debate about the documents that are not pro- duced, whether reviewed or simply discarded as likely irrelevant, but that is a different debate.

This point recently received judicial acknowledgement in an opinion issued by U.S. Magistrate Judge Andrew J. Peck, *Rio Tinto PLC v. Vale S.A.*, 2015 BL 54331 (S.D.N.Y. 2015).

Discussing the broader issue of transparency with respect to the training sets used in TAR, Judge Peck observed that CAL minimizes the need for transparency.

If the TAR methodology uses "continuous active learning" (CAL) (as opposed to simple passive learning (SPL) or simple active learning (SAL)), the contents of the seed set is much less significant.

Let's see how this works, comparing a typical TAR 1.1 to a TAR 2.0 process.

TAR 1.0: One-Time Training Against a Control Set

Control Set

Seed Set

SME

TRAIN

TEST

Rank All Documents and Establish Cutoff

Transfer to Review Platform

Collect / Receive

A Typical TAR 1.0 Review Process. As depicted, a TAR 1.0 review is built around the following steps:

1. A subject matter expert (SME), often a senior lawyer, reviews and tags a sample of randomly selected documents (usually about 500) to use as a "control set" for training.

2. The SME then begins a training process often starting with a seed set based on hot documents found through keyword searches.

3. The TAR engine uses these judgments to build a classification/ranking algorithm that will find other relevant documents. It tests the algorithm against the 500- document control set to gauge its accuracy.

4. Depending on the testing results, the SME may be asked to do more training to help improve the classification/ranking algorithm. This may be through a review of random or computer-selected documents.

5. This training and testing process continues until the classifier is "stable." That means its search algorithm is no longer getting better at identifying relevant documents in the control set.

Once the classifier has stabilized, training is complete. At that point your TAR engine has learned as much about the control set as it can. The next step is to turn it loose to rank the larger document population (which can take hours to complete) and then divide the documents into categories to review or not.

Importance of Control Set. In such a process, you can see why emphasis is placed on the development of the 500-document control set and the subsequent training. The control set documents are meant to represent a much larger set of review documents, with every document in the control set standing in for what may be a thousand review documents. If one of the control documents is improperly tagged, the algorithm might suffer as a result.

Of equal importance is how the subject matter expert tags the training documents. If the training is based on only a few thousand documents, every decision could have an important impact on the outcome. Tag the documents improperly and you might end up reviewing a lot of highly ranked irrelevant documents or missing a lot of lowly ranked relevant ones.

TAR 2.0 Continuous Learning; Ranking All Documents Every Time

TAR 2.0 systems don't use a control set for training. Rather, they rank all of the review documents every time on a continuous basis. Modern TAR engines don't require hours or days to rank a million documents. They can do it in minutes, which is what fuels the continuous learning process.

A TAR 2.0 engine can continuously integrate new judgments by the review team into the analysis as their work progresses. This allows the review team to do the training rather than depending on an SME for this purpose.

It also means training is based on tens or hundreds of thousands of documents, rather than rely on a few thousand seen by the expert before review begins.

TAR 2.0: Continuous Active Learning Model

As the infographic demonstrates, the CAL process is easy to understand and simple to administer. In effect, the reviewers become the trainers and the trainers be- come reviewers. Training is review, we say. And review is training.

CAL Steps.

1. Start with as many seed documents as you can find. These are primarily relevant documents which can be used to start training the system. This is an optional step to get the ranking started but is not required. It may involve as few as a single relevant document or many thousands of them.

2. Let the algorithm rank the documents based on your initial seeds.

3. Start reviewing documents based in part on the initial ranking.

4. As the reviewers tag and release their batches, the algorithm continually takes into account their feedback. With increasing numbers of training seeds, the system gets smarter and feeds more relevant documents to the review team.

5. Ultimately, the team runs out of relevant documents and stops the process. We confirm that most of the relevant documents

have been found through a systematic sample of the entire population. This allows us to create a yield curve as well so you can see how effective the system was in ranking the documents.

What Does This Have to Do With Transparency?

In a TAR 2.0 process, transparency is no longer a problem because training is integrated with review. If opposing counsel asks to see the "seed" set, the answer is simple: "You already have it."

Every document tagged as relevant is a seed in a continuous review process. And every relevant non- privileged document will be or has been produced.

Likewise, there is no basis to look over the expert's shoulder during the initial training because there is no expert doing the training. Rather, the review team does the training and continues training until the process is complete. Did they mis-tag the training documents? Take a look and see for yourself.

This eliminates the concern that you will disclose work product through transparency. With CAL, all of the relevant documents are produced, as they must be with no undue emphasis placed on an initial training set. The documents, both good and bad, are there in the production for opposing counsel to see. But work product or individual judgments by the producing party are hidden. Voila, the transparency problem goes away.

Postscript: What About Other Disclosure Issues?

Discard Pile Issues. In addressing the transparency concern, I don't mean to suggest there are no other disclosure issues to be addressed. For example, with any TAR process that uses a review cutoff, there is always concern about the discard pile. How does one prove that the discard pile can be ignored as not having a significant number of relevant documents?

That is an important issue, one that we discuss in Chapter 7 of this book.

The problem doesn't go away with TAR 2.0 and CAL, but it is the same issue advocates have to address in a TAR 1.0 process as well. This requires sampling as I explain in my two measuring recall articles referenced above.

Tagging for Non-Relevance; Collection. What about documents tagged as non-relevant by the review team? How do I know that was done properly?

This too is a separate issue that exists in both TAR 1.0 and 2.0 processes. Indeed, it also exists with linear re- view.

And, last but not least, did I properly collect the documents submitted to the TAR process? Good question but, again, a question that applies whether you use TAR or not. Unless you collect the right documents, no process will be reliable.

Again, these are issues to be addressed in a different article. They exist in whichever TAR process you choose to use. My point here is that with a TAR 2.0 process, a number of the "transparency" issues that bug people and have hindered the use of this amazing process simply go away.

This chapter reproduced with permission from Digital Discovery & e-Evidence, *15 DDEE 110, 03/19/2015. Copyright @ 2015 by The Bureau of National Affairs, Inc. (800-372-1033) http://www. bna.com*

10

TAR 2.0: Continuous Ranking

Is One Bite at the Apple Really Enough?

For all of its complexity, technology assisted review (TAR) in its traditional form is easy to sum up:

1. A lawyer (subject matter expert) sits down at a computer and looks at a subset of documents.

2. For each, the lawyer records a thumbs-up or thumbs-down decision (tagging the document). The TAR algorithm watches carefully, learning during this training.

3. When training is complete, we let the system rank and divide the full set of documents between (predicted) relevant and irrelevant.[1]

4. We then review the relevant documents, ignoring the rest.

The benefits from this process are easy to see. Let's say you started with a million documents that otherwise would have to be reviewed by your team. If the computer algorithm predicted with the requisite degree of confidence that 700,000 are likely non-relevant, you could then exclude them from the review for a huge savings in review costs. That is a great result, particularly if you are the one paying the bills.

But is that it? Once you "part the waters" after the document ranking, you are stuck reviewing the 300,000 that fall on the relevant side of the cutoff. If I were the client, I would wonder whether there were steps you could take to reduce the document population even further. While reviewing 300,000 documents is better than a million, cutting that to 250,000 or fewer would be even better.

Can We Reduce the Review Count Even Further?

The answer is yes, if we can change the established paradigm. TAR 1.0 was about the benefits of identifying a cutoff point after running a training process using a subject matter expert (SME). TAR 2.0 is about continuous ranking throughout the review process—using review teams as well as SMEs. As the review teams work their way through the documents, their judgments are fed back to the computer algorithm to further improve the ranking. As the ranking improves, the cutoff point is likely to improve as well. That means even fewer documents to review, at a lower cost. The work gets done more quickly as well.

It Can Be as Simple as That!

Insight Predict is built around this idea of continuous ranking. While you can use it to run a traditional TAR process, we encourage clients to take more than one bite at the ranking apple. Start the training by finding as many relevant documents (responsive, privileged, etc.) as your team can identify. Supplement these documents (often called seeds) through random sampling, or use our contextual diversity sampling to view documents selected for their distinctiveness from documents already seen.[2]

The computer algorithm can then use these training seeds as a basis to rank your documents. Direct the top-ranked ones to the review team for their consideration.

In this scenario, the review team starts quickly, working from the top of the ranked list. As they review documents, you feed their judgments back to the system to improve the ranking, supplemented with other training documents chosen at random or through contextual diversity. Meanwhile, the review team continues to draw from the highest-ranked documents, using the most recent ranking available. They continue until the review is complete.[3]

Does It Work?

Logic tells us that continuously updated rankings will produce better results than a one-time process. As you add more training documents, the algorithm should improve. At least, that is the case with the Catalyst platform. While rankings based on a few thousand training documents can be quite good, they almost always improve through the addition of more training documents. As our Senior Research Scientist Jeremy Pickens says: "More is more." And more is better.

And while more is better, it does not necessarily mean more work for the team. Our system's ability to accept additional training documents, and to continually refine its rankings based on those additional exemplars, results in the review team having to review fewer documents, saving both time and money.

Testing the Hypothesis

We decided to test our hypothesis using three different review projects. Because each had already gone through linear review, we had what Dr. Pickens calls "ground truth" about all of the records being ranked. Put another way, we already knew whether the documents were responsive or privileged (which were the goals of the different reviews).[4]

Thus, in this case we were not working with a partial sample or drawing conclusions based on a sample set. We could run the ranking process as if the documents had not been reviewed but then match up the results to the actual tags (responsive or privileged) given by the reviewers.

The Process

The tests began by picking six documents at random from the total collection. We then used those documents as training seeds for an initial ranking. We then ranked all of the documents based on those six exemplars.[5]

From there, we simulated delivering new training documents to the reviewers. We included a mix of highly ranked and random documents, along with others selected for their contextual diversity (meaning they were different from anything previously selected for training). We used this technique to help ensure that the reviewers saw a diverse range of documents—hopefully improving the ranking results.

Our simulated reviewers made judgments on these new documents based on tags from the earlier linear review. We then submitted their judgments to the algorithm for further training and ranking. We continued this train-rank-review process, working in batches of 300, until we reached an appropriate recall threshold for the documents.

What do I mean by that? At each point during the iteration process, Insight Predict ranked the entire document population. Because we knew the true responsiveness of every document in the collection, we could easily track how far down in the ranking we would have to go to cover 50%, 60%, 70%, 80%, 90%, or even 95% of the relevant documents.

From there, we plotted the information to compare how many documents you would have to review using a one-time ranking process versus a continuous ranking approach. For clarity and simplicity, I chose two recall points to display: 80% (a common recall level) and 95% (high but achievable with our system). I could have presented several other recall rates as well but it might make the charts more confusing than necessary. The curves all looked similar in any event.

The Research Studies

Below are charts showing the results of our three case studies. These charts are different from the typical yield curves because they serve a different purpose. In this case, we were trying to demonstrate the efficacy of a continuous ranking process rather than a single ranking outcome.

Specifically, along the X-axis is the number of documents that were manually tagged and used as seeds for the process (the simulated review process). Along the Y-axis is the number of documents the review team would have to review (based on the seeds input to that point) to reach a desired recall level. The black diagonal line crossing the middle represents the simulated review counts, which were being continually fed back to the algorithm for additional training.

This will all make more sense when I walk you through the case studies. The facts of these cases are confidential, as are the clients and actual case names. But the results are highly interesting to say the least.

Research Study One: Wellington F Matter (Responsive Review)

This case involved a review of 85,506 documents. Of those, 11,460 were judged responsive. That translates to a prevalence (richness) rate of about 13%. Here is the resulting chart from our simulated review:

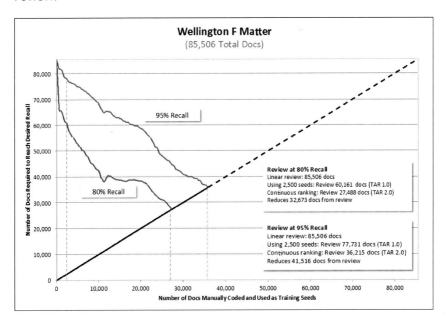

There is a lot of information on this chart so I will take it step by step. The black diagonal line represents the number of seeds given to our virtual reviewers. It starts at zero and continues along a linear path until it intersects the 95% recall line. After that, the line becomes dashed to reflect the documents that might be included in a linear review but would be skipped in a TAR 2.0 review.

The red line represents the number of documents the team would have to review to reach the 80% recall mark. By that I simply mean that after you reviewed that number of documents, you would have seen 80% of the relevant documents in the population. The counts (from the Y axis) range from a starting point of 85,506 documents at zero seeds (essentially a linear review)[6] to 27,488 documents (intersection with the black line) if you used continuous review.

I placed a grey dashed vertical line at the 2,500 document mark This figure is meant to represent the number of training documents you might use to create a one-time ranking for a traditional TAR 1.0 process.[7] Some systems require a larger number of seeds for this process but the analysis is essentially the same.

Following the dashed grey line upwards, the review team using TAR 1.0 would have to review 60,161 documents to reach a recall rate of 80%. That number is lower than the 85,000+ documents that would be involved with a linear review. But it is still a lot of documents and many more than the 27,488 required using continuous ranking.

With continuous ranking, we would continue to feed training documents to the system and continually improve the yield curve. The additional seeds used in the ranking are represented by the black diagonal line as I described earlier. It continues upwards and to the right as more seeds are reviewed and then fed to the ranking system.

The key point is that the black solid line intersects the red 80% ranking curve at about 27,488 documents. At this point in the review, the review team would have seen 80% of the relevant documents in the collection. We know this is the case because we have the reviewer's judgments on all of the documents. As I mentioned earlier, we treated those judgments as "ground truth" for this research study.[8]

What Are the Savings?

The savings come from the reduction of documents required to reach the 80% mark. By my calculations, the team would be able to reduce its review burden from 60,161 documents in the TAR 1.0 process to 27,488 documents in the TAR 2.0 process—a reduction of another 32,673 documents. That translates to an additional 38% reduction in review attributable to the continuous ranking process. That is not a bad result. If you figure $4 a document for review costs,[9] that would come to about $130,692 in additional savings.

It is worth mentioning that total savings from the TAR process are even greater. If we can reduce the total document population from 85,506 to 28,000 documents, that represents a reduction of 58,018 documents, or about 68%. At $4 a document, the total savings from the TAR process comes to $232,072.

We would be missing the boat if we stopped the analysis here. We all know the old expression, "Time is money." In this case, the time savings from continuous ranking over a one-time ranking can be just as important as the savings on review costs. If we assumed your reviewer could go through 50 documents an hour, the savings for 80% recall would be a whopping 653 hours of review time avoided. At eight hours per review day, that translates to 81 review days saved.[10]

How About for 95% Recall?

If you followed our description of the ranking curve for 80% recall, you can see how we would come out if our goal were to achieve 95% recall. We have placed a summary of the numbers in the chart but we will recap them here.

1. Using 2,500 seeds and the ranking at that point, the TAR 1.0 team would have to review 77,731 documents in order to reach the 95% recall point.

2. With TAR 2.0's continuous ranking, the review team could drop the count to 36,215 documents for a savings of 41,516 documents. That comes to a 49% savings.

3. At $4 a document, the savings from using continuous ranking instead of TAR 1.0 would be $166,064. The total savings over linear review would be $202,024.

4. Using our review metrics from above, this would amount to
    saving 830 review hours or 103 review days.

The bottom line on this case is that continuous ranking saves a
substantial amount on both review costs and review time.

Research Study Two: Ocala M Matter (Responsive Review)

This case involved a review of 57,612 documents. Of those, 11,037
were judged relevant. That translates to a prevalence rate of about
19%, a bit higher than in the Wellington F Matter.

Here is the resulting chart from our simulated review.

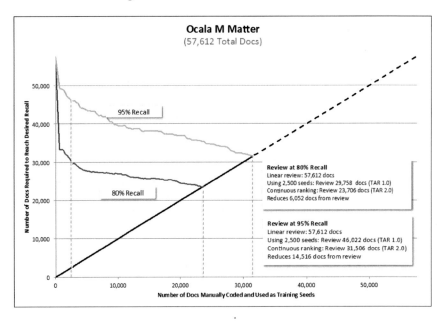

For an 80% recall threshold, the numbers are these:

1. Using TAR 1.0 with 2,500 seeds and the ranking at that point, the
    team would have to review 29,758 documents in order to reach
    the 80% recall point.

2. With TAR 2.0 and continuous ranking, the review team could drop
    the count to 23,706 documents for a savings of 6,052 documents.
    That would be an 11% savings.

3. At $4 a document, the savings from the continuous ranking process would be $24,208.

Compared to linear review, continuous ranking would reduce the number of documents to review by 33,906, for a cost savings of $135,624.

For a 95% recall objective, the numbers are these:

1. Using 2,500 seeds and the ranking at that point, the TAR 1.0 team would have to review 46,022 documents in order to reach the 95% recall point.

2. With continuous ranking, the TAR 2.0 review team could drop the count to 31,506 documents for a savings of 14,516 documents. That comes to a 25% savings.

3. At $4 a document, the savings from the continuous ranking process would be $58,064.

Not surprisingly, the numbers and percentages in the Ocala M study are different from the numbers in Wellington F, reflecting different documents and review issues. However, the underlying point is the same. Continuous ranking can save a substantial amount on review costs as well as review time.

Research Study Three: Wellington F Matter (Privilege Review)

The team on the Wellington F Matter also conducted a privilege review against the 85,000+ documents. We decided to see how the continuous ranking hypothesis would work for finding privileged documents. In this case, the collection was sparse. Of the 85,000+ documents, only 983 were judged to be privileged. That represents a prevalence rate of just over 1%, which is relatively low and can cause a problem for some systems.

Here is the resulting chart using the same methodology:

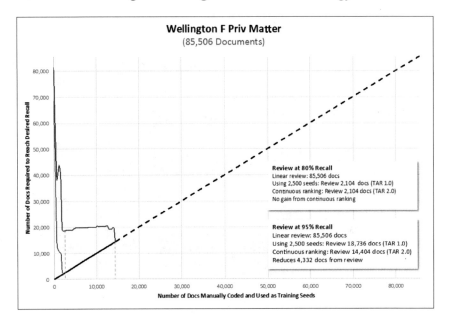

Wellington F Priv Matter
(85,506 Documents)

For an 80% recall threshold, the numbers are these:

1. The TAR 1.0 training would have finished the process after 2,104 training seeds. The team would have hit the 80% recall point at that time.

2. There would be no gain from continuous ranking in this case because the process would be complete during the initial training.

The upshot from this study is that the team would have saved substantially over traditional means of reviewing for privilege (which would involve linear review of some portion of the documents).[11] However, there were no demonstrative savings from continuous ranking.

We recognize that most attorneys would demand a higher threshold than 80% for a privilege review. For good reasons, they would not be comfortable with allowing 20% of the privileged documents to slip through the net. The 95% threshold might bring them more comfort.

For a 95% recall objective, the numbers are these:

1. Using 2,500 seeds and the ranking at that point, the TAR 1.0 team would have to review 18,736 documents in order to reach the 95% recall point.

2. With continuous ranking, the TAR 2.0 review team could drop the count to 14,404 documents for a savings of 4,332 documents.

3. At $4 a document, the savings from the continuous ranking process would be $17,328.

For actual privilege reviews, we recommend that our clients use many of the other analytics tools in Insight to make sure that confidential documents don't fall through the net. Thus, for the documents that are not actually reviewed during the TAR 2.0 process, we would be using facets to check the names and organizations involved in the communications to help make sure there is no inadvertent production.

What About the Subject Matter Experts?

In reading this, some of you may wonder what the role of a subject matter expert might be in a world of continuous ranking. Our answer is that the SME's role is just as important as it was before but the work might be different. Instead of reviewing random documents at the beginning of the process, SMEs might be better advised to use their talents to find as many relevant documents as possible to help train the system. Then, as the review progresses, SMEs play a key role doing QC on reviewer judgments to make sure they are correct and consistent. Our research suggests that having experts review a portion of the documents tagged by the review team can lead to better ranking results at a much lower cost than having the SME review all of the training documents.

Ultimately, a continuous ranking process requires that the review team carry a large part of the training responsibility as they do their work. This sits well with most SMEs who don't want to do standard review work even when it comes to relatively small training sets. Most senior lawyers that I know have no desire to review the large numbers of documents that would be required to achieve the benefits of continuous ranking. Rather, they typically want to review as few documents as possible. "Leave it to the review team," we often hear. "That's their job."

Conclusion

As these three research studies demonstrate, continuous ranking can produce better results than the one-time ranking approach associated with traditional TAR. These cases suggest that potential savings can be as high as 49% over the one-time ranking process.

As you feed more seeds into the system, the system's ability to identify responsive documents continues to improve, which makes sense. The result is that review teams are able to review far fewer documents than traditional methods require and achieve even higher rates of recall.

Traditional TAR systems give you one bite at the apple. But if you want to get down to the core, one bite won't get you there. Continuous ranking lets one bite feed on another, letting you finish your work more quickly and at lower cost. One bite at the apple is a lot better than none, but why stop there?

Footnotes

1. Relevant in this case means relevant to the issues under review. TAR systems are often used to find responsive documents but they can be used for other inquiries such as privileged, hot or relevant to a particular issue.

2. Catalyst's contextual diversity algorithm is designed to find documents that are different from those already seen and used for training. We use this method to ensure that we aren't missing documents that are relevant but different from the mainstream of documents being reviewed.

3. Determining when the review is complete is a subject for another day. Suffice it to say that once you determine the appropriate level of recall for a particular review, it is relatively easy to sample the ranked documents to determine when that recall threshold has been met.

4.   We make no claim that a test of three cases is anything more than a start of a larger analysis. We didn't hand pick the cases for their results but would readily concede that more case studies would be required before you could draw a statistical conclusion. We wanted to report on what we could learn from these experiments and invite others to do the same.

5.   Catalyst's system ranks all of the documents each time we rank. We do not work off a reference set (i.e. a small sample of the documents).

6.   We recognize that IR scientists would argue that you only need to review 80% of the total population to reach 80% recall in a linear review. We could use this figure in our analysis but chose not to simply because the author has never seen a linear review that stopped before all of the documents were reviewed—at least based on an argument that they had achieved a certain recall level as a result of reaching a certain threshold. Clearly you can make this argument and are free to do so. Simply adjust the figures accordingly.

7.   This isn't a fair comparison. We don't have access to other TAR systems to see what results they might have after ingesting 2,500 seed documents. Nor can we simulate the process they might use to select those seeds for the best possible ranking results. But it is the data I have to work with. The gap between one-time and continuous ranking may be narrower but I believe the essential point is the same. Continuous ranking is like continuous learning: the more of it the better.

8.   In a typical review, the team would not know they were at the 80% mark without testing the document population. We know in this case because we have all the review judgments. In the real world, we recommend the use of a systematic sample to determine when target recall is being approached by the review.

9.   We chose this figure as a placeholder for the analysis. We have seen higher and lower figures depending on who is doing the review. Feel free to use a different figure to reflect your actual review costs.

10.   We used 50 documents per hour as a placeholder for this calculation. Feel free to substitute different figures based on your experience. But saving on review costs is only half the benefit of a TAR process.

11.   Most privilege reviews are not linear in the sense that all documents in a population are reviewed. Typically, some combination of searches is run to identify the likely privileged candidates. That number should be smaller than the total but can't be specified in this exercise.

11

Subject Matter Experts

What Role Should They Play in TAR 2.0 Training?

If you accept the cost-saving benefits of continuous ranking, you are all but forced to ask about the role of experts. Most experts (often senior lawyers) don't want to review training documents, even though they may acknowledge the value of this work in cutting review costs. They chafe at clicking through random and often irrelevant documents and put off the work whenever possible.

Often, this holds up the review process and frustrates review managers, who are under pressure to get moving as quickly as possible. New uploads are held hostage until the reluctant expert can come back to the table to review the additional seeds. Indeed, some see the need for experts as one of the bigger negatives about the TAR process.

Continuous ranking using experts would be a non-starter. Asking senior lawyers to review 3,000 or more training documents is one thing.[1] Asking them to continue the process through 10,000, 50,000 or even more documents could lead to early retirement–yours, not theirs. "I didn't go to law school for that kind of work," they'll say. "Push it down to the associates or those contract reviewers we hired. That's their job."

So, our goal was to find out how important experts are to the training process, particularly in a TAR 2.0 world. Are their judgments essential to ensure optimal ranking or can review team judgments be just as effective? Ultimately, we wondered if experts could work hand in hand with the review team, doing tasks better suited to their expertise, and achieve better and faster training results—at less cost than using the expert exclusively for the training. Our results were interesting, to say the least.

Research Population

We used data from the 2010 TREC program[2] for our analysis. The TREC data is built on a large volume of the ubiquitous Enron documents, which we used for our ranking analysis. We used judgments about those documents (i.e. relevant to the inquiry or not) provided by a team of contract reviewers hired by TREC for that purpose.

In many cases, we also had judgments on those same documents made by the topic authorities on each of the topics for our study. This was because the TREC participants were allowed to challenge the judgments of the contract reviewers. Once challenged, the document tag would be submitted to the appropriate topic authority for further review. These were the people who had come up with the topics in the first place and presumably knew how the documents should be tagged. We treated them as SMEs for our research.

So, we had data from the review teams and, often, from the topic authorities themselves. In some cases, the topic authority affirmed the reviewer's decision. In other cases, they were reversed. This gave us a chance to compare the quality of the document ranking based on the review team decisions and those of the SMEs.[3]

Methodology

We worked with the four TREC topics from the legal track. These were selected essentially at random. There was nothing about the documents or the results that caused us to select one topic over the other. In each case, we used the same methodology I will describe here.

For each topic, we started by randomly selecting a subset of the overall documents that had been judged. Those became the training documents, sometimes called seeds. The remaining documents were used as evaluation (testing) documents. After we developed a ranking based on the training documents, we could test the efficacy of that ranking against the actual review tags in the larger evaluation set.[4]

As mentioned earlier, we had parallel training sets, one from the reviewers and one from the SMEs. Our random selection of documents for training included documents on which both the SME and a basic reviewer agreed, along with documents on which the parties disagreed. Again, the selection was random so we did not control how much agreement or disagreement there was in the training set.

Experts vs. Review Teams: Which Produced the Better Ranking?

We used Insight Predict to create two separate rankings. One was based on training using judgments from the experts. The other was based on training using judgments from the review team. Our idea was to see which training set resulted in a better ranking of the documents.

We tested both rankings against the actual document judgments, plotting our results in standard yield curves. In that regard, we used the judgments of the topic authorities to the extent they differed from those of the review team. Since they were the authorities on the topics, we used their judgments in evaluating the different rankings. We did not try to inject our own judgments to resolve the disagreement.

Using the Experts to QC Reviewer Judgments

As a further experiment, we created a third set of training documents to use in our ranking process. Specifically, we wanted to see what impact an expert might have on a review team's rankings if the expert were to review and "correct" a percentage of the review team's judgments. We were curious whether it might improve the overall rankings and how that effort might compare to rankings done by an expert or review team without the benefit of a QC process.

We started by submitting the review team's judgments to Predict. We then asked Predict to rank the documents in this fashion:

1. The lowest-ranked positive judgments (reviewer tagged it relevant while Predict ranked it highly non-relevant); and

2. The highest-ranked negative judgments (reviewer tagged it non-relevant while Predict ranked it highly relevant).

The goal here was to select the biggest outliers for consideration. These were documents where our Predict ranking system most strongly differed from the reviewer's judgment, no matter how the underlying documents were tagged.

We simulated having an expert look at the top 10% of these training documents. In cases where the expert agreed with the reviewer's judgments, we left the tagging as is. In cases where the expert had overturned the reviewer's judgment based on a challenge, we reversed the tag. When this process was finished, we ran the ranking again based on the changed values and plotted those values as a separate line in our yield curve.

Plotting the Differences: Expert vs. Reviewer Yield Curves

A yield curve presents the results of a ranking process and is a handy way to visualize the difference between two processes. The X-axis shows the percentage of documents that are reviewed. The Y-axis shows the percentage of relevant documents found at each point in the review.

Here were the results of our four experiments.

Issue One

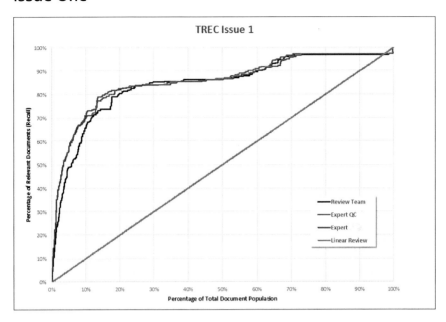

The lines above show how quickly you would find relevant documents during your review. As a base line, we created a gray diagonal line to show the progress of a linear review (which essentially moves through the documents in random order). Without a better basis for ordering of the documents, the recall rates for a linear review typically match the percentage of documents actually reviewed— hence the straight line. By the time you have seen 80% of the documents, you probably have seen 80% of the relevant documents.

The blue, green and red lines are meant to show the success of the rankings for the review team, expert and the use of an expert to QC a portion of the review team's judgments. Notice that all of the lines are above and to the left of the linear review curve. This means that you could dramatically improve the speed at which you found relevant documents over a linear review process with any of these ranking methods. Put another way, it means that a ranked review approach would present more relevant documents at any point in the review (until the end). That is not surprising because TAR is typically more effective at surfacing relevant documents than linear review.

In this first example, the review team seemed to perform at a less effective rate than the expert reviewer at lower recall rates (the blue curve is below and to the right of the other curves). The review team ranking would, for example, require the review of a slightly higher percentage of documents to achieve an 80% recall rate than the expert ranking.[5] Beyond 80%, however, the lines converge and the review team seems to do as good a job as the expert.

When the review team was assisted by the expert through a QC process, the results were much improved. The rankings generated by the expert-only review were almost identical to the rankings produced by the review team with QC assistance from the expert. We will show later that this approach would save you both time and money, because the review team can move more quickly than a single reviewer and typically bills at a much lower rate.

Issue Two

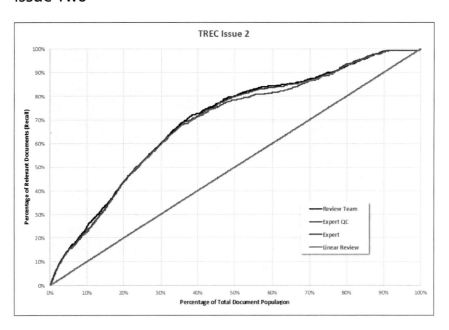

In this example, the yield curves are almost identical, with the rankings by the review team being slightly better than those of an expert alone. Oddly, the expert QC rankings drop a bit around the 80% recall line and stay below until about 85%. Nonetheless, this experiment shows that all three methods are viable and will return about the same results.

Issue Three

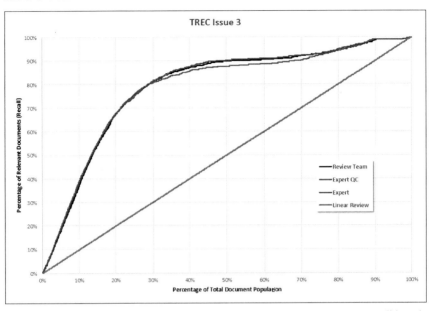

In this case the ranking lines are identical until about the 80% recall level. At that point, the expert QC ranking process drops a bit and does not catch up to the expert and review team rankings until about 90% recall. Significantly, at 80% recall, all the curves are about the same. Notice that this recall threshold would only require a review of 30% of the documents, which would suggest a 70% cut in review costs and time.

Issue Four

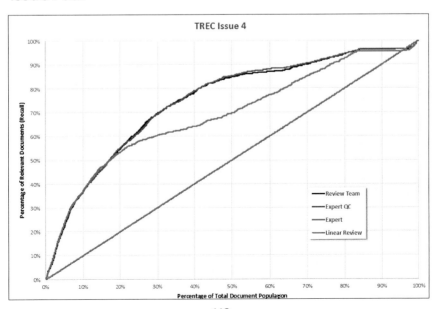

Issue four offers a somewhat surprising result and may be an outlier. In this case, the expert ranking seems substantially inferior to the review team or expert QC rankings. The divergence starts at about the 55% recall rate and continues until about 95% recall. This chart suggests that the review team alone would have done better than the expert alone. However, the expert QC method would have matched the review team's rankings as well.

What Does This All Mean?

That's the million-dollar question. Let's start with what it doesn't mean. These were tests using data we had from the TREC program. We don't have sufficient data to prove anything definitively but the results sure are interesting. It would be nice to have additional data involving expert and review team judgments to extend the analysis.

In addition, these yield curves came from our product, Insight Predict. We use a proprietary algorithm that could work differently from other TAR products. It may be that experts are the only ones suitable to train some of the other processes. Or not.

That said, these yield curves suggest strongly that the traditional notion that only an expert can train a TAR system may not be correct. On average in these experiments, the review teams did as well or better than the experts at judging training documents. We believe it provides a basis for further experimentation and discussion.

Why Does This Matter?

There are several reasons this analysis matters. They revolve around time and money.

First, in many cases, the expert isn't available to do the initial training, at least not on your schedule. If the review team has to wait for the expert to get through 3,000 or so training documents, the delay in the review can present a problem. Litigation deadlines seem to get tighter and tighter. Getting the review going more quickly can be critical in some instances.

Second, having review teams participate in training can cut review costs. Typically, the SME charges at a much higher billing rate than a reviewer. If the expert has to review 3,000 training documents at a higher billable rate, total costs for the review increase accordingly. Here is a simple chart illustrating the point.

Expert Only	Hourly	Review Rate	Documents	Total	Time Spent
1 Expert	$550	60	3,000	$27,500	50

Expert and Review Team	Hourly	Review Rate	Documents	Total	Time Spent
10 Reviewers	$60	60	3,000	$3,000	5.0
1 Expert	$550	60	300	$2,750	5.0
				$5,750	10.0

Total Savings				$21,750	40.0

Using the assumptions we have presented, having an expert do all of the training would take 50 hours and cost almost $27,500. In contrast, having a review team do most of the training while the expert does a 10% QC, will reduce the cost by 85%, to $5,750. The time spent on the combined review process changes from 50 hours (6+ days) to 10 combined hours, a bit more than a day.[6]

You can use different assumptions for this chart but the point is the same. Having the review team involved in the process saves time and money. Our testing suggests that this happens with no material loss to the ranking process.

This all becomes mandatory when you move to continuous ranking. The process is based on using the review team rather than an expert for review. Any other approach would not make sense from an economic perspective or be a good or desirable use of the expert's time.

So what should the expert do in a TAR 2.0 environment? We suggest that experts do what they are trained to do (and have been doing since our profession began). Use the initial time to interview witnesses and find important documents. Feed those documents to the ranking system to get the review started. Then use the time to QC the review teams and to search for additional good documents. Our research so far suggests that the process makes good sense from both a logical and efficiency standpoint.

Footnotes

1. Typical processes call for an expert to train about 2,000 documents before the algorithm "stabilizes." They also require the expert to review 500 or more documents to create a control set for testing the algorithm and a similar amount for testing the ranking results once training is complete. Insight Predict does not use a control set (the system ranks all the documents with each ranking). However, it would require a systematic sample to create a yield curve.

2. The Text Retrieval Conference is sponsored by the National Institute for Standards and Technology. (http://trec.nist.gov/)

3. We aren't claiming that this perfectly modeled a review situation but it provided a reasonable basis for our experiments. In point of fact, the SME did not re-review all of the judgments made by the review team. Rather, the SME considered those judgments where a vendor appealed a review team assessment. In addition, the SMEs may have made errors in their adjudication or otherwise acted inconsistently. Of course that can happen in a real review as well. We just worked with what we had.

4. Note that we do not consider this the ideal workflow. A completely random seed set, with no iteration and no judgmental/automated seeding, this test does not (and is not intended to) create the best yield curve. Our goal here was to put all three tests on level footing, which this methodology does.

5. In this case, you would have to review 19% of the documents to achieve 80% recall for the ranking based only on the review team's training and only 14% based on training by an expert.

6. We used "net time spent" for the second part of this chart to illustrate the real impact of the time saved. While the review takes a total of 55 hours (50 for the team and 5 for the expert), the team works concurrently. Thus, the team finishes in just 5 hours, leaving the expert another 5 hours to finish his QC. The training gets done in a day (or so) rather than a week.

12

Comparing Active Learning to Random Sampling

Using Zipf's Law to Evaluate Which is More Effective for TAR

In 2014, Maura Grossman and Gordon Cormack recently released a blockbuster article, "Comments on 'The Implications of Rule 26(g) on the Use of Technology-Assisted Review,'" 7 Fed. Cts. L. Rev. 286 (2014). 7 Fed. Cts. L. Rev. 286 (2014). The article was in part a response to an earlier article in the same journal by Karl Schieneman and Thomas Gricks, in which they asserted that Rule 26(g) imposes "unique obligations" on parties using TAR for document productions and suggested using techniques we associate with TAR 1.0 including:

> *Training the TAR system using a random "seed" or "training" set as opposed to one relying on judgmental sampling, which "may not be representative of the entire population of electronic documents within a given collection."*

From the beginning, we have advocated a TAR 2.0 approach that uses judgmental seeds (selected by the trial team using all techniques at their disposal to find relevant documents). Random seeds are a convenient shortcut to approximating topical coverage, especially when one doesn't have the algorithms and computing resources to model the entire document collection. But they are neither the best way to train a modern TAR system nor the only way eliminate bias and ensure full topical coverage. We have published several research papers and articles showing that documents selected via continuous active learning and contextual diversity (active modeling of the entire document set) consistently beat training documents selected at random.

In this latest article and in a recent peer-reviewed study, Cormack and Grossman also make a compelling case that random sampling is one of the least effective methods for training. Indeed, they conclude that even the worst examples of keyword searches are likely to bring better training results than random selection, particularly for populations with low levels of richness.

Ralph Losey has also written on the issue at his *e-Discovery Team* blog, arguing that relying on random samples rather than judgmental samples "ignores an attorney's knowledge of the case and the documents. It is equivalent to just rolling dice to decide where to look for something, instead of using your own judgment, your own skills and insights."

Our experience, like theirs, is that judgmental samples selected using attorneys' knowledge of the case can get you started more effectively, and that any possible bias arising from the problem of "unknown unknowns" can be easily corrected with the proper tools. We also commonly see document collections with very low richness, which makes these points even more important in actual practice.

Herb Roitblat, the developer of OrcaTec (which apparently uses random sampling for training purposes), believes in the superiority of a random-only sampling approach. His main argument is that training using judgmental seeds backed by review team judgments leads to "bias" because "you don't know what you don't know." Our experience, which is now backed by the peer-reviewed research of Cormack and Grossman, is that there are more effective ways to avoid bias than simple random sampling.

We certainly agree with Roitblat that there is always a concern for "bias," at least in the sense of not knowing what you don't know. But it isn't necessarily a problem that prevents us from ever using judgmental seeds. Sometimes—depending on the skill, knowledge, and nature of the relevant information in the matter itself—judgmental selection of training documents can indeed cover all relevant aspects of a matter. At other times, judgmental samples will miss some topics because of the problem of "unknown unknowns" but this deficiency can be easily corrected by using an algorithm such as contextual diversity that models the entire document population and actively identifies topics that need human attention rather than blindly relying on random samples to hit those pockets of documents the attorneys missed.

The goal of this post, however, is not to dissect the arguments on either side of the random sampling debate. Rather, we want to have a bit of fun and show you how Zipf's law and the many ways it is manifest in document populations argue strongly for the form of active learning we use to combat the possibility of bias. Our method is called "contextual diversity" and Zipf's law can help you understand why it is more efficient and effective than random sampling for ensuring topical coverage and avoiding bias.

What is Contextual Diversity?

A typical TAR 1.0 workflow often involves an expert reviewing a relatively small set of documents, feeding those documents into the TAR system to do its thing, and then having a review team check samples to confirm the machine's performance. But in TAR 2.0, we continuously use all the judgments of the review teams to make the algorithm smarter (which means you find relevant documents faster). Like Cormack and Grossman, we feed documents ranked high for relevance to the review team and use their judgments to train the system. However, our continuous learning approach also throws other options into the mix to further improve performance, combat potential bias, and ensure complete topical coverage. One of these options that addresses all three concerns is our "contextual diversity" algorithm.

Contextual diversity refers to documents that are highly different from the ones already seen and judged by human reviewers (and thus under a TAR 2.0 approach have been used in training), no matter how those documents were initially selected for review. Because our system ranks all of the documents in the collection on a continual basis, we know a lot about documents—both those the review team has seen but also (and more importantly) those the review team has not yet seen. The contextual diversity algorithm identifies documents based on how significant and how different they are from the ones already seen, and then selects training documents that are the most representative of those unseen topics for human review.

It's important to note that the algorithm doesn't know what those topics mean or how to rank them. But it can see that these topics need human judgments on them and then select the most representative documents it can find for the reviewers. This accomplishes two things: (1) it is constantly selecting training documents that will provide the algorithm with the most information possible from one attorney-document view, and (2) it is constantly putting the next biggest "unknown unknown" it can find in front of attorneys so they can judge for themselves whether it is relevant or important to their case.

We feed in enough of the contextual diversity documents to ensure that the review team gets a balanced view of the document population, regardless of how any initial seed documents were selected. But we also want the review team focused on highly relevant documents, not only because this is their ultimate goal, but also because these documents are highly effective at further training the TAR system as Cormack and Grossman now confirm. Therefore, we want to make the contextual diversity portion of the review as efficient as possible. How we optimize that mix is a trade secret, but the concepts behind contextual diversity and active modeling of the entire document population are explained below.

Contextual Diversity: Explicitly Modeling the Unknown

In the following example, assume you started the training with contract documents found either through keyword search or witness interviews. You might see terms like the ones above the blue dotted line showing up in the documents. Documents 10 and 11 have human judgments on them (indicated in red and green), so the TAR system can assign weights to the contract terms (indicated in dark blue).

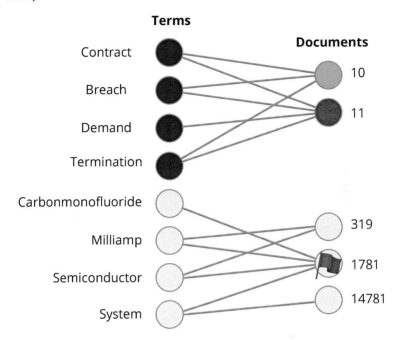

But what if there are other documents in the collection, like those shown below the dotted line, that have highly technical terms but few or none of the contract terms? Maybe they just arrived in a rolling collection. Or maybe they were there all along but no one knew to look for them. How would you find them based on your initial terms? That's the essence of the bias argument.

With contextual diversity, we analyze all of the documents. Again, we're not solving the strong artificial intelligence problem here, but the machine can still plainly see that there is a pocket of different, unjudged documents there. It can also see that one document in particular, 1781, is the most representative of all those documents, being at the center of the web of connections among the unjudged terms and unjudged documents. Our contextual diversity engine would therefore select that one for review, not only because it gives the best "bang for the buck" for a single human judgment, but also because it gives the attorneys the most representative and efficient look into that topic that the machine can find.

So Who is This Fellow Named Zipf?

Zipf's law was named after the famed American linguist George Kingsley Zipf, who died in 1950. The law refers to the fact that many types of data, including city populations and a host of other things studied in the physical and social sciences, seem to follow a Zipfian distribution, which is part of a larger family of power law probability distributions. (You can read all about Zipf's law in Wikipedia, where we pulled this description.)

Why does this matter? Bear with us, you will see the fun of this in just a minute.

It turns out that the frequency of words and many other features in a body of text tend to follow a Zipfian power law distribution. For example, you can expect the most frequent word in a large population to be twice as frequent as the second most common word, three times as frequent as the third most common word and so on down the line. Studies of Wikipedia itself have found that the most common word, "the," is twice as frequent as the next, "of," with the third most frequent word being "and." You can see how the frequency drops here:

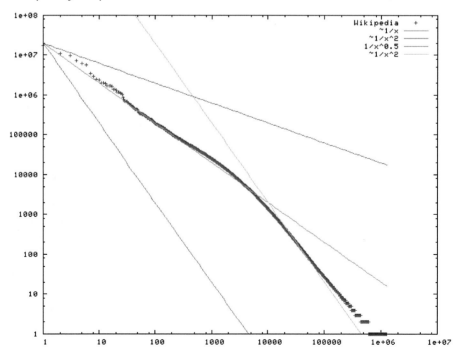

Topical Coverage and Zipf's Law

Here's something that may sound familiar: Ever seen a document population where documents about one topic were pretty common, and then those about another topic were somewhat less common, and so forth down to a bunch of small, random stuff? We can model the distribution of subtopics in a document collection using Zipf's law too. And doing so makes it easier to see why active modeling and contextual diversity is both more efficient and more effective than random sampling.

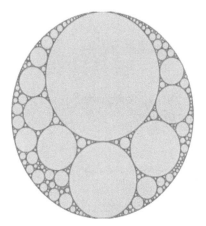

Here is a model of our document collection, broken out by subtopics. The subtopics are shown as bubbles, scaled so that their areas follow a Zipfian distribution. The biggest bubble represents the most prevalent subtopic, while the smaller bubbles reflect increasingly less frequent subtopics in the documents.

Now to be nitpicky, this is an oversimplification. Subtopics are not always discrete, boundaries are not precise, and the modeling is much too complex to show accurately in two dimensions. But this approximation makes it easier to see the main points.

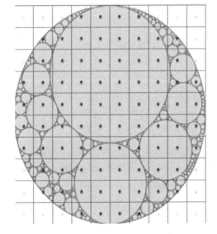

So let's start by taking a random sample across the documents, both to start training a TAR engine and also to see what stories the collection can tell us.

We'll assume that the documents are distributed randomly in this population, so we can draw a grid across the model to represent a simple random sample. The red dots reflect each of 80 sample documents. The portion of the grid outside the circle is ignored.

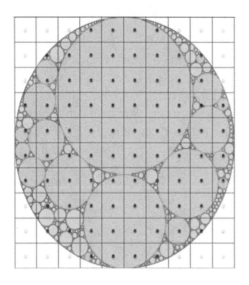

We can now represent our topical coverage by shading the circles covered by the random sample.

You can see that a number of the randomly sampled documents hit the same topical circles. In fact, over a third (32 out of 80) fall in the largest subtopic. A full dozen are in the next largest. Others hit some of the smaller circles, which is a good thing, and we can see that we've colored a good proportion of our model yellow with this sample.

So in this case, a random sample gives fairly decent results without having to do any analysis or modeling of the entire document population. But it's not great. And with respect to topical coverage, it's not exactly unbiased, either. The biggest topics have a ton of representation, a few tiny ones are now represented by a full 1/80 of the sample, and many larger ones were completely missed. So a random sample has some built-in topical bias that varies randomly—a different random sample might have biases in different directions. Sure, it gives you some rough statistics on what is more or less common in the collection, but both attorneys and TAR engines usually care more about what is in the collection rather than how frequently it appears.

So what if we actually can perform analysis and modeling of the entire document population? Can we do better than a random sample? Yes, as it turns out, and by quite a bit.

Let's attack the problem again by putting attorney eyes on 80 documents—the exact same effort as before—but this time we select the sample documents using a contextual diversity process. Remember: our mission is to find representative documents from as many topical groupings as possible to train the TAR engine most effectively, avoid any bias that might arise from judgmental sampling, and to help the attorneys quickly learn everything they need to from the collection. Here is the topical coverage achieved using contextual diversity for the the same size review set of 80 documents:

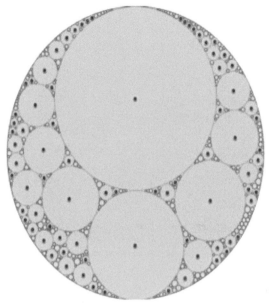

Now look at how much of that collection is colored yellow. By actively modeling the whole collection, the TAR engine with contextual diversity uses everything it can see in the collection to give reviewing attorneys the most representative document it can

find from each subtopic. By using its knowledge of the documents to systematically work through the subtopics, it avoids massively oversampling the larger ones and relying on random samples to eventually hit all the smaller ones (which, given the nature of random samples, need to be very large to have a decent chance of hitting all the small stuff). It achieves much broader coverage for the exact same effort.

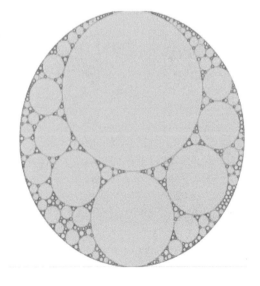

At right is a comparison of the two different approaches to selecting a sample of 80 documents. The subtopics colored yellow were covered by both. Orange indicates those that were found using contextual diversity but missed by the random sample of the same size. Dark blue shows those smaller topics that the random sample hit but contextual diversity did not reach in the first 80 seed documents.

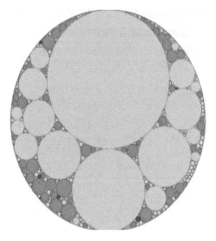

Finally, here is a side by side comparison of the topical coverage achieved for the same amount of review effort:

Random   **Contextual Diversity**

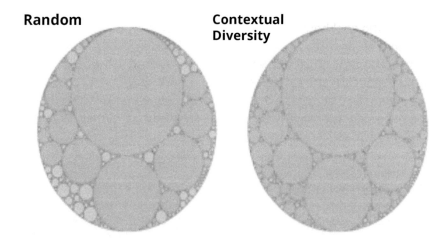

Now imagine that the attorneys started with some judgmental seeds taken from one or two topics. You can also see how contextual diversity would help balance the training set and keep the TAR engine from running too far down only one or two paths at the beginning of the review by methodically giving attorneys new, alternative topics to evaluate.

When subtopics roughly follow a Zipfian distribution, we can easily see how simple random sampling tends to produce inferior results compared to an active learning approach like contextual diversity. (In fact, systematic modeling of the collection and algorithmic selection of training documents beats random sampling even if every topic were the exact same size, but for other reasons we will not go into here).

For tasks such as a review for production where the recall and precision standards are based on "reasonableness" and "proportionality," random sampling—while not optimal—may be good enough. But if you're looking for a needle in a haystack or trying to make sure that the attorneys' knowledge about the collection is complete, random sampling quickly falls farther and farther behind active modeling approaches.

So while we strongly agree with the findings of Cormack and Grossman and their conclusions regarding active learning, we also know through our own research that the addition of contextual diversity to the mix makes the results even more efficient.

After all, the goal here is to find relevant documents as quickly and efficiently as possible while also quickly helping attorneys learn everything they need to know to litigate the case effectively. George Zipf is in our corner.

13

Using TAR in International Litigation

Does Predictive Coding Work for Non-English Languages?

A 2014 U.S. Department of Justice memorandum questioned the effectiveness of using technology assisted review with non-English documents. The fact is that, done properly, TAR can be just as effective for non-English as it is for English documents.

This is true even for the so-called "CJK languages," Asian languages including Chinese, Japanese and Korean. Although these languages do not use standard English-language delimiters such as spaces and punctuation, they are nonetheless candidates for the successful use of technology assisted review.

The DOJ memorandum, published on March 26, 2014, addresses the use of TAR by the Antitrust Division. The author, Tracy Greer, senior litigation counsel for electronic discovery, acknowledges that TAR "offers the promise of reducing the costs" for parties responding to a DOJ second request in a proposed merger or acquisition.

Even so, Greer questions whether TAR would be effective with non-English documents. "In investigations in which TAR has been employed, we have not been entirely satisfied that the TAR process works effectively with foreign- and mixed-language documents," she writes. While the division "would be open to discussion" about using TAR in such cases, she adds, it is not ready to adopt it as a standard procedure.

This is an important issue, not just for antitrust but for litigation and regulatory matters across the board. As the world gets flatter, legal matters increasingly encompass documents in multiple languages. Greer notes this in the antitrust context, writing, "As the division's investigations touch more international companies, we have seen a substantial increase in foreign-language productions."

To be fair, the DOJ is not alone in questioning TAR's effectiveness for non-English documents. Many industry professionals share that doubt. They perceive TAR as a process that involves "understanding" documents. If the documents are in a language the system does not understand, then TAR cannot be effective, they reason.

Of course, computers don't actually "understand" anything (so far, at least). TAR programs simply catalog the words in documents and apply mathematical algorithms to identify relationships among them. To be more precise, we call what they recognize "tokens," because often the fragments are not even words, but numbers, acronyms, misspellings or even gibberish.

The question, then, is whether computers can recognize tokens (words or otherwise) when they appear in other languages. The simple answer is yes. If the documents are processed properly, TAR can be just as effective for non-English as it is for English documents.

TAR for Non-English Documents

To understand why TAR can work with non-English documents, you need to know two basic points:

1. TAR doesn't understand English or any other language. It uses an algorithm to associate words with relevant or irrelevant documents.

2. To use the process for non-English documents, particularly those in Chinese and Japanese, the system has to first tokenize the document text so it can identify individual words.

We will hit these topics in order.

1. TAR Doesn't Understand English

It is beyond the province of this article to provide a detailed explanation of how TAR works, but a basic explanation will suffice for our purposes. Let me start with this: TAR doesn't understand English or the actual meaning of documents. Rather, it simply analyzes words algorithmically according to their frequency in relevant documents compared to their frequency in irrelevant documents.

Think of it this way: We train the system by marking documents as relevant or irrelevant. When I mark a document relevant, the computer algorithm analyzes the words in that document and ranks them based on frequency, proximity or some other such basis. When I mark a document irrelevant, the algorithm does the same, this time giving the words a negative score. At the end of the training process, the computer sums up the analysis from the individual training documents and uses that information to build a search against a larger set of documents.

While different algorithms work differently, think of the TAR system as creating huge searches using the words developed during training. It might use 10,000 positive terms, with each ranked for importance. It might similarly use 10,000 negative terms, with each ranked in a similar way. The search results would come up in an ordered fashion sorted by importance, with the most likely relevant ones coming first.

None of this requires that the computer know English or the meaning of the documents or even the words in them. All the computer needs to know is which words are contained in which documents.

2. If Documents Are Properly Tokenized, the TAR Process Will Work

Tokenization may be an unfamiliar term to you but it is not difficult to understand. When a computer processes documents for search, it pulls out all of the words and places them in a combined index. When you run a search, the computer doesn't go through all of your documents one by one. Rather, it goes to an ordered index of terms to find out which documents contain which terms. That's why search works so quickly. Even Google works this way, using huge indexes of words.

As we mentioned, however, the computer doesn't understand words or even that a word is a word. Rather, for English documents it identifies a word as a series of characters separated by spaces or punctuation marks. Thus, it recognizes the words in this sentence because each has a space (or a comma) before and after it. Because not every group of characters is necessarily an actual "word," information retrieval scientists call these groupings "tokens," and the act of identifying these tokens for the index as "tokenization."

All of these are tokens:

- Bank

- door

- 12345

- barnyard

- mixxpelling

And so on. All of these will be kept in a token index for fast search and retrieval.

Certain languages, such as Chinese and Japanese, don't delineate words with spaces or western punctuation. Rather, their characters run through the line break, often with no breaks at all. It is up to the reader to tokenize the sentences in order to understand their meaning.

Many early English-language search systems couldn't tokenize Asian text, resulting in search results that often were less than desirable. More advanced search systems, like the one we chose for Catalyst, had special tokenization engines which were designed to index these Asian languages and many others that don't follow the Western conventions. They provided more accurate search results than did their less-advanced counterparts.

Similarly, the first TAR systems were focused on English-language documents and could not process Asian text. At Catalyst, we added a text tokenizer to make sure that we handled these languages properly. As a result, our TAR system can analyze Chinese and Japanese documents just as if they were in English. Word frequency counts are just as effective for these documents and the resulting rankings are as effective as well.

A Case Study to Prove the Point

Let us illustrate this with an example from a matter we handled not long ago. We were contacted by a major U.S. law firm that was facing review of a set of mixed Japanese and English language documents. It wanted to use TAR on the Japanese documents, with the goal of cutting both the cost and time of the review, but was uncertain whether TAR would work with Japanese.

Our solution to this problem was to first tokenize the Japanese documents before beginning the TAR process. Our method of tokenization—also called segmentation—extracts the Japanese text and then uses language-identification software to break it into words and phrases that the TAR engine can identify.

To achieve this, we loaded the Japanese documents into our review platform. As we loaded the documents, we performed language detection and extracted the Japanese text. Then, using our proprietary technology and methods, we tokenized the text so the system would be able to analyze the Japanese words and phrases.

With tokenization complete, we could begin the TAR process. In this case, senior lawyers from the firm reviewed 500 documents to create a reference set to be used by the system for its analysis. Next, they reviewed a sample set of 600 documents, marking them relevant or non-relevant. These documents were then used to train the system so it could distinguish between likely relevant and likely non-relevant documents and use that information for ranking.

After the initial review, and based on the training set, we directed the system to rank the remainder of the documents for relevance. The results were compelling:

- The system was able to identify a high percentage of likely relevant documents (98%) and place them at the front of the review queue through its ranking process. As a result, the review team would need to review only about half of the total document population (48%) to cover the bulk of the likely relevant documents.

- The remaining portion of the documents (52%) contained a small percentage of likely relevant documents. The review team reviewed a random sample from this portion and found only 3% were likely relevant. This low percentage suggested that these documents did not need to be reviewed, thus saving the cost of reviewing over half the documents.

By applying tokenization before beginning the TAR process, the law firm was able to target its review toward the most-likely relevant documents and to reduce the total number of documents that needed to be reviewed or translated by more than half.

Conclusion

As corporations grow increasingly global, legal matters are increasingly likely to involve non-English language documents. Many believed that TAR was not up to the task of analyzing non-English documents. The truth, however, is that with the proper technology and expertise, TAR can be used with any language, even difficult Asian languages such as Chinese and Japanese.

Whether for English or non-English documents, the benefits of TAR are the same. By using computer algorithms to rank documents by relevance, lawyers can review the most important documents first, review far fewer documents overall, and ultimately cut both the cost and time of review. In the end, that is something their clients will understand, no matter what language they speak.

14

Case Study: Major Bank Slashes Review Costs with Innovative E-Discovery Technology

Catalyst's Insight Predict Cuts Production Review Costs by 94%

Our client was a large banking institution embroiled in nasty litigation with a now-defunct borrower. The bank alleged it lost millions due to the borrower's principals' accounting fraud. Legal shots were fired, excuses ran rampant and the parties went hard at each other to see where the blame would end up. Bring on the discovery.

The Problem

Responding to a production request, our client conducted an extensive investigation to find responsive documents. Even after using a variety of techniques to cull those that it found, it was still left with over 2.1 million that needed consideration. Further keyword searching might have resulted in more reductions but the team wasn't comfortable with what that process might miss.

Realizing they had neither the time nor money to review all 2.1 million documents, client and counsel turned to Insight Predict, Catalyst's unique technology assisted review (TAR) engine. The plan was to employ Predict's continuous active learning (CAL) protocol and see if TAR might be effective in further reducing the population in a defensible manner.

Step One: Building a Seed Set

In this case, counsel had already reviewed and identified approximately 50,000 relevant documents for a previous production based on a similar request. Because our predictive ranking engine has no effective limit on the amount of training seeds it can handle, we used these documents as initial seeds to start the ranking process. Almost immediately, relevant documents from the larger collection were pushed to the front of the line for review.

Step Two: Immediate Review

Reviews using first-generation TAR 1.0 systems cannot begin until senior lawyers (aka subject matter experts) train the system. With Insight Predict's advanced TAR 2.0 technology, this is not necessary. Rather, the review team could immediately begin requesting batches of documents to review.

Predict's algorithm provided batches made up primarily of the documents it most highly ranked. This ensured that the review team was productive immediately, because they were focused on the documents that were most likely relevant. In turn, it enabled the trial team to quickly get their hands on the most important documents to help sharpen their analysis of the case.

The review batches also included a mix of documents chosen based on their "contextual diversity." This unique feature of Insight is designed to solve the problem of "you don't know what you don't know." Specifically, our contextual diversity algorithm chooses documents for review that are different than those already reviewed.

In effect, the algorithm clusters unseen documents by their common themes. It then pulls the most relevant examples from each cluster and presents them to reviewers as part of the batch. If the reviewer tags an example as relevant, the ranking engine is cued to promote similar documents. If the example is not relevant, the ranking engine learns that this cluster is of lesser interest.

The ultimate goal of the CAL protocol is to feed reviewer judgments back to the system to improve the training and thereby the responsiveness rate for subsequent review assignments. As the reviewers release their batches, Insight Predict adds their judgments to further its training. The net result is that the algorithm gets smarter and smarter about finding and promoting relevant documents. This is in sharp contrast to the "one-time" training used by the earlier TAR 1.0 systems.

Step Three: Using Keyword Search to Further Improve the Training

Predict's ability to use flexible inputs allowed the review team to take a multimodal approach to finding responsive documents. As the review progressed, Predict identified promising search terms as well as custodians who held the most likely relevant documents.

This enabled the trial team independently to run searches with these key terms and then tag the relevant documents found through their searches.

As with the regular review, these tagged documents could then be fed into Predict's ranking engine to further improve the training. This way, every attorney judgment on a document was used by Predict, no matter where that judgment was made.

Step Four: Completing the Review

Early on in the review, we took a richness sample to get a feel for the number of relevant documents to expect in the collection. That sample suggested we would find one relevant document out of every 100, which translates to a richness estimate of 1%.

As the review progressed, we tracked the number of relevant

documents found by the team. Toward the beginning, the team tagged 10% relevant, representing a ten-fold increase in review productivity. Over time, that figure rose to 25% and sometimes as high as 35%. Through their tagging, the review team showed that the predictive ranking process was paying dividends.

Eventually, the relevant documents petered out, dropping down to and below base richness. At this point the team decided to stop the review and measure their progress.

Step Five: Measuring the Results

To determine how many relevant documents the team had found, we ran a systematic random sample against the entire document population. In this case the team chose to sample just under 6,000 documents, which is larger than the typical discovery sample. The goal was to present results with a high level of confidence and a narrow margin of error. Senior attorney reviewers manually reviewed these documents for added credibility.

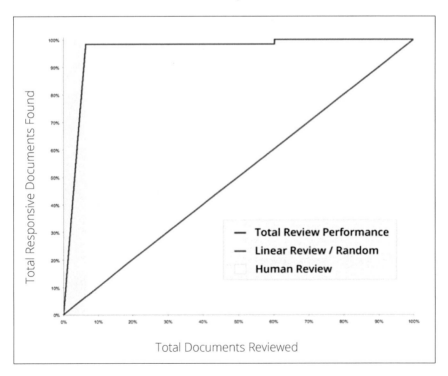

Conclusion: 98% Recall After Reviewing Just 6.4% of the Total Population

The sample suggested that the team had found and reviewed 98% of the documents relevant to the production. This conclusion was based on a sample confidence level of 95% and a 2% margin of error. Even taking the lower end of the margin-of-error range, we estimated that the team had found at least 92% of the relevant documents, still well beyond levels previously approved by the courts.

All of this was accomplished through a CAL workflow that put attorney reviewers' eyes on every document produced, yet still required a total review effort of only 6.4% of the total reviewable population of 2.1 million documents. That was 1.97 million documents the attorneys were saved from having to review.

15

Government Regulator Uses Predict to Cut Review By 59%

How Insight Predict Succeeded Where Keywords Failed

When the regulatory agency sued the private company, it sought to recover over $1 million the company had allegedly overbilled the government. But when the short-staffed agency faced a tight discovery deadline in the case, it knew there was not time for manual review. Turning to Insight Predict, Catalyst's second-generation technology assisted review platform, the agency was able to cut its review nearly 60%.

The Problem: Short-Staffed Agency Faces Tight Production Deadline

The agency's lawsuit alleged improper billing practices by the company. The company sought discovery of documents relating a number of issues, including communications between the parties, the investigation process, notification procedures and software licensing.

The court gave the agency five weeks to produce documents. After collection and culling, the agency had 79,000 documents left to review. Working with a limited budget, it had only five part-time reviewers to do the job. The deadline was too tight for linear review.

Selecting Insight Predict to Bridge the Gap

After reviewing several TAR providers, the agency decided on Catalyst's Insight Predict and its advanced continuous active learning (CAL) protocol. The agency concluded that CAL offered it a number of advantages over earlier TAR methods including:

- Every attorney decision gets used in training;

- Rolling collections do not require starting over;

- Review teams do the training, subject matter experts not required;

- Ranking is continuous with no interruptions to review;

In addition, independent research showed that CAL was more effective in finding relevant documents than first generation of TAR products .

The CAL Protocol Enabled A Rapid Start for the Review

From an earlier review, the agency had 11,000 documents it had already tagged as relevant or not. With the CAL protocol, these documents could be used for initial training and to create a starting ranking for the review. That ranking took only a few minutes and, once it was complete, the team immediately launched into the review.

The team reviewed batches of 20 documents for each round, automatically fed to them by Insight Predict. As they tagged and released the documents, their judgments were fed back to the predictive ranking algorithm to further train the system. As the training progressed, Insight Predict continuously reranked the documents to further improve the batches sent to the review team.

With each batch, the algorithm continued to improve, moving more and more responsive documents to the front of the queue.

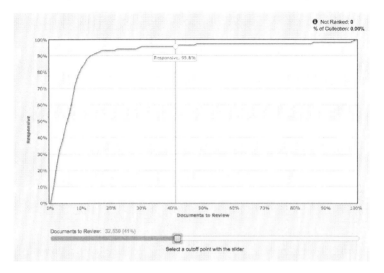

Taking a Sample to Analyze the Results

When the batches stopped producing relevant documents, the team stopped review. At that point, we took a systematic random sample to determine how many relevant documents had been reviewed. The sample was large, encompassing 1,500 documents for a confidence level of 98% and a 3% margin of error.

Using those results, Insight generated the yield curve seen above. It showed that the team had found over 95% of the relevant documents after reviewing just 41% of the document population.

Conclusion: Its Review Reduced By 59%, the Agency Met its Deadline

With just five weeks and a small staff to review 79,000 documents, the agency faced a challenge. By using Insight Predict, it not only avoided the cost of reviewing 59% of the population, but it also sharply reduced overall review time.

The bottom line was that the agency met its deadlines without exceeding its budget. For the agency, that made for a double win.

16

Using TAR 2.0 to Streamline Document Review for Japanese Patent Litigation

Continuous Active Review Cuts Cost by Over 85%

Our client was a multinational Japanese company facing a large document production in an international patent dispute. The initial review collection exceeded 2 million documents. After a series of rolling uploads, which continued throughout the review, the population slated for review grew to 3.6 million. Facing millions in review costs, the client sought an alternative to linear review.

Review time was short. The client's goal was to finish the review in four weeks with a small team handling the project. The documents were primarily in Japanese, with some English in the mix, and many involved highly technical subject matter.

Estimating Richness and Training

Even though the client had taken steps to remove junk and other documents not subject to production, the collection's estimated richness was still miniscule. An initial systematic random sample of 1,000 documents (97% confidence with a 3.5% margin of error) suggested that there were fewer than six relevant documents in every thousand that might be presented through a linear review. As is often the case in litigation, richness was low at 0.6%.

Before Catalyst was engaged, a team of lawyers had reviewed about 10,000 documents found through keyword search. For many TAR 1.0 engines, which have a limited training phase, these judgments would have been of no use. Because Catalyst's technology, Insight Predict, is a TAR 2.0 engine that uses continuous learning and continuous ranking, we could make use of these judgments as initial training seeds.

As you can see from the below yield curve, the initial training using the 10,000 seeds proved effective. It indicated that almost all of the relevant documents could be found after reviewing just 17% of the total review population. This meant that the review team could immediately exclude most of the non-relevant documents and start finding relevant documents many times faster than the day before. There was no need for the team to spend non- productive hours looking at largely irrelevant files selected randomly for initial training.

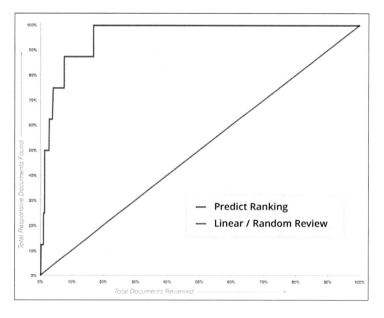

Optimizing Review with Continuous Active Learning

The initial training worked. Richness in the documents presented to the review team jumped from 0.6% to as much as 35%, which represented a 60-fold improvement in review efficiency. At the same time, the reviewers received a mix of documents selected for "contextual diversity." This feature, integrated into Predict, allows the algorithm to keep finding and training against documents which are different from those already found through keyword search or seen by the reviewers in their initial rounds. You can read more about our unique contextual diversity algorithm on our website.

The review continued while the collection team added more documents. Since Predict can continually rank all the documents in the collection, there is no problem adding new documents during the review. As they are added, the documents are ranked and mixed into the total collection. To the extent they are similar to already ranked documents, they join the ranking in their proper place. To the extent they are different than what has already been collected, they become candidates for contextual diversity and can be included in the review sets for hands-on evaluation by the reviewers.

TAR 1.0 systems typically train against a reference set, which makes handling rolling collections difficult. To be representative, the reference set must be chosen randomly from the entire population and then carefully tagged by a subject matter expert. Then the training process begins with each round being measured by Its effectiveness against the reference set.

If new documents are collected during the TAR 1.0 process, you have two options, with neither being ideal. Either you hope/assume that the new documents are similar to those already collected. Or you start again, discarding the initial reference set and its related training for a new round.

Rolling Collections and Continuous Learning

As mentioned earlier, through rolling collections over the course of several weeks, the Predict population grew to 3.6 million unique, rankable documents. As the review team found new types of responsive documents and learned more about the case, they could also use any other search and analytics tools available to keep searching. Every decision they made was continuously fed back into Predict to improve its ranking. When the review team ran out of relevant documents, they stopped the review and conducted a further systematic random sample of the entire population. Here is what they learned:

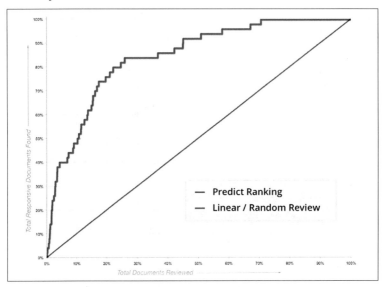

As you can see from the resulting yield curve, Predict was still pushing relevant documents to the top of the review pile, even after multiple rolling collections were added while the review was in progress.

Ultimately, the total review effort was about 500,000 documents, out of 3.6 million scheduled for review. Predict allowed the review team to achieve the requisite recall after reviewing only a small fraction of the population, which met the client's needs for both speed and efficiency. The team is now using Predict to help organize the review of all in-bound productions from other parties.

Tokenizing Japanese Documents

In the early days of technology assisted review (TAR), many questioned whether it was suitable for Japanese and other Asian-language documents. Indeed, for most TAR 1.0 engines, the answer was, and perhaps still is, a resounding "No." After all, these products were designed to work on English-language documents that use spaces and punctuation to define word boundaries. For languages that do not follow Western syntax, the systems could not build the indexes required for them to work.

It is important to note that TAR systems don't actually understand the words they index and analyze. Rather they employ mathematical algorithms to determine the frequency and use of the words both in the documents and across the document population.

Japanese and other languages that do not use spaces between words often have to be "tokenized" (broken out into artificial words) before they can be indexed for search and analytics tools. Many earlier tools do this in a simple way, just taking two or three characters at a time. While this approach works okay for basic search, it can make analysis very difficult for TAR 1.0 systems.

TAR 2.0 systems such as Insight Predict employ special software to tokenize Japanese and similar languages a smarter way. They are able to analyze the text and break out actual words and word phrases, not just arbitrary groups of characters. Once the Japanese documents were properly tokenized, the TAR 2.0 process could index and analyze them more effectively.

Conclusion

This case presented a number of challenges. The collection was mostly in Japanese and contained a number of highly technical documents. The richness of the collection was low and it contained a lot of junk. The client was on a tight timeline for review but collections kept arriving on a rolling basis.

Despite these challenges, we were able to make use of the 10,000 documents the legal team had already reviewed to jumpstart the ranking process and accelerate the review. Even with the collection's low richness, the team was able to find highly relevant documents many times faster than with any other approach. And because Predict never stopped learning from newly-reviewed documents, it continued to improve and help attorneys explore the collection even as new documents were constantly being added.

In the end, using Predict and its ability to support continuous active learning, the client was able to cut the time and cost of its review by over 85%.

Postscript: A Supplemental Review

Because of continuing collections in the case, another 132,000 documents were loaded after we finished the final systematic random sample. But because we could use the existing judgments and Predict training, our client was able to get through that last batch of stragglers quickly.

The review of that late-arriving batch had to have a separate validation procedure performed to support the decision to stop the review when the review team no longer saw relevant documents.

The procedure showed that the estimated recall on that last batch was 87%, even higher than the recall for the much larger, master collection that had accumulated over the rest of the review.

17

Case Study: Predict Proves Effective for Small Collection

Facing Tight Deadline in SEC Probe, Company Reduces Review by 75%

The question has persisted since technology assisted review got its start. How big does a case need to be before it makes sense to load it into a TAR system? Are 10,000 documents enough? How about 100,000? In this case, it was just 16,000 documents, but TAR enabled the company to cut its review by 75% and get it done in under a week.

The Problem: A Tight Deadline and a Fixed Budget

Our client was a major law firm representing a company in an SEC investigation on a fixed-fee basis. It had a relatively small document set to review—just 16,000 documents. But the deadline was tight, the review had to be done quickly, and the company did not want to use contract attorneys, preferring instead to have the firm's own lawyers take the laboring oar.

With So Small a Set, Would TAR Make Sense?

Mindful of its tight deadline, the firm wanted to use Insight Predict, our TAR 2.0 predictive ranking engine, to find the relevant documents more quickly. But it was concerned that using TAR with so few documents would be costly and ineffective.

With a first-generation TAR 1.0 system, the concern would have been justified. With TAR 1.0, they would need a senior lawyer to serve as subject matter expert to start the training process. The SME would first have to review and tag 500 or more randomly selected documents as a control set to use for measuring training efforts. Then the SME would have to do multiple rounds of training before the review could even begin.

This might require review of 1,600 or more documents before the system stabilized. Depending on the case, the training could require review of many more documents, easily as many as 3,000.

After that, the SME would have to tag an additional sample, perhaps another 500 documents, just to test whether the training was complete. All told, the SME might have to review 3,000 to 4,000 documents just to train the TAR 1.0 classifier. Only then could the review begin.

That's a lot of work for a case with a small number of documents. It is why many e-discovery professionals advise that TAR should only be used for larger cases. Some suggest the threshold is 100,000 documents before you can justify the SME's training efforts and expense.

Insight Predict Requires No Control Set or SME

With Insight Predict, the size of the collection is not a factor. With Predict's continuous active learning protocol, there is no minimum threshold because there is no need to create a control set. Predict ranks all of the documents all of the time. Predict does not require an SME to do the initial training. With no need for an SME, the review team can get started right away. Review is training and training is review.

In this case, the CAL process was quick and simple to implement. The team initially found 67 relevant documents through keyword search. We used these as training seeds for the initial ranking. Then the team started reviewing documents.

It turned out that about 11% of the documents were relevant, for a total of about 1,800 relevant documents. As the team reviewed documents, Predict continuously learned from their tagging and presented increasingly relevant batches to the reviewers. Relevance 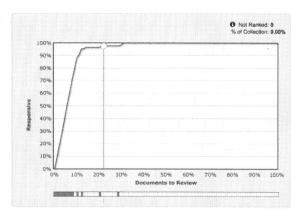 in the batches quickly rose to as high as 70%. Review efficiency increased seven-fold as a result.

In just days, batch relevance dropped to single digits as the team depleted the relevant population. The team stopped review and moved to a systematic sample to determine what level of recall was obtained. The sample involved 800 documents for a confidence level of 98% and a 4% margin of error. By this point, the team had reviewed just 3,900 documents.

The sample showed the team had found 96% of the relevant documents after reviewing only 25% of the population. The remaining documents could be safely discarded cutting out 75% of the review time and costs.

Conclusion: Insight Predict is Effective Even for Small Collections

Does TAR work for smaller cases? With Insight Predict and continuous active learning, the size of the collection does not matter. In this case, the team used Predict to finish their review in less than a week. They easily met the SEC's deadline while also keeping well within their fixed-fee budget.

18

Case Study: Patent Case Proves It's Never Too Late to Use TAR

Even After Manually Reviewing Half the Collection, TAR Produced Substantial Savings

"It's never too late," people often say. But is that true for technology assisted review? If a legal team has already put substantial time and effort into manual review, can TAR still be worthwhile? That was the issue presented in a patent infringement case where the client's approval to use TAR came only after the law firm had manually reviewed nearly half the collection. Even that late in the game, Insight Predict produced substantial savings in time and cost.

The Problem: Having to Start the Review before Getting the OK for TAR

The law firm represented a generic pharmaceutical manufacturer that had been sued for patent infringement by a major brand-name pharmaceutical company. The plaintiff claimed that our client's generic products infringed its patents.

The total collection to be reviewed (after applying search terms and culling) numbered about 40,800 documents. While not a huge collection, it was nevertheless a lot of documents to get through and would be a significant expense for the client.

Believing that TAR would enable them to get through the review more quickly and at less cost, the lawyers recommended it to the client. But looming deadlines demanded that they get started on the review even as the client considered the recommendation. It was only after the firm had manually reviewed nearly half the collection that it received the client's approval to proceed with TAR.

The Benefit: A Jump Start from the Documents Already Reviewed

By the time the approval came in, the firm had already reviewed some 18,200 of the 40,800 total documents. Had they used TAR from the outset, they likely would have avoided reviewing even that many documents. Even so, those documents gave them the advantage of providing a ready-made set of seeds to use to train the TAR algorithm.

Catalyst used the coding determinations from those 18,200 documents to train Insight Predict, its next-generation TAR engine. Predict uses continuous active learning, a machine-learning protocol that enables it to use any and all previously coded documents as judgmental seeds to start the process. This means that there are not separate workflows for training the TAR system and for review, as was the case with first-generation TAR 1.0 systems. All documents that already have attorney decisions on them can be fed into the system at the start, and the entire population is analyzed and ranked.

After that first ranking was complete, Predict was set to automatically create batches of 50 records each. Each batch contained the next-best, unreviewed documents most likely responsive to the opposing party's production request. Each batch also included a few "contextually diverse" documents to make sure there are no topics or concepts in the collection that go unexplored by reviewers.

As the reviewers completed their batches, the system continuously re-ranked the entire population in the background, incorporating their new coding calls to "get smarter" and improve its predictions. Each time a reviewer clicked a button for more documents, the system created a new batch based on the most recently completed re-ranking.

The Result: TAR Cuts the Remaining Review by 70%

The review proceeded along this track until the reviewers started seeing batches with few, if any, relevant documents. This was an indication that few relevant documents remained. The results were tested by sampling the unreviewed documents. Statistical analysis showed that the review had achieved a very high "recall"— meaning that the team had found the vast majority of the relevant documents.

By the end of the TAR process, the team had reviewed another 6,800 documents, beyond the initial 18,200. There remained another 15,800 documents that they never had to review. That meant that, once they started using TAR, they had to review only 30% of the remaining documents. TAR saved 70% of the remaining expense and time the review would have otherwise required.

By the standards of some large cases, these numbers may not sound like a huge savings. But a 70% savings on even a portion of a larger review can be significant. In this case, the law firm calculated that using TAR saved the client more than $70,000, even after accounting for the cost of TAR.

The Conclusion: Even Midway Through a Review, TAR Had a Substantial Impact

Even when started midway through a relatively small but technical review, TAR's impact can still be dramatic. It was only after manually reviewing nearly half the documents that the team switched to using TAR. Even then, by using TAR, the team was able to eliminate the need to manually review 70% of the remaining documents and 40% of the entire set. That resulted in substantial cost savings to the client and time savings to the litigation team.

19

Case Study: Using Insight Predict for Review of Rolling Productions

Insight Predict Finds 75% of Hot Docs While Cutting Review 92%

Finding "hot" documents in an opposing party's production is rarely easy. But when those productions are large and arrive on a rolling basis, the search can be even more cumbersome, costly and time-consuming.

This was the scenario faced by plaintiffs in a lawsuit alleging predatory home-lending practices by a major financial institution. However, through the use of Insight Predict, the only technology assisted review platform on the market that uses continuous active learning (CAL), coupled with Catalyst's unique contextual diversity sampling, the plaintiffs were able to reduce the number of documents they had to review by 92%.

Challenge: Find Hot Documents in Opponent's Rolling Productions

The plaintiffs in this case were working with limited resources to take on a major financial institution. In response to the plaintiffs' discovery requests, the defendant had started to produce large numbers of electronic documents, with the productions arriving in waves on a rolling basis.

To prepare for depositions and further litigation, the plaintiffs had to quickly find the hot documents within these productions. But with limited resources, they could not afford to review them all manually.

Solution: Use Insight Predict to Create Prioritized Review

Two features of Insight Predict made it ideally suited to this case. First was continuous active learning, which gives it the ability to handle rolling productions. Because Predict ranks every document every time, new documents can be added continuously. This differs from earlier TAR platforms, which train against a small reference set and are therefore limited in their ability to handle rolling uploads.

Second, Predict differs from other platforms in its ability to effectivelyhandle document populations with low richness (a low prevalence of relevant documents). In this case, when we evaluated the initial population of the defendant's produced documents, we estimated that only about 1% were hot. For other platforms, that would have been a problem.

By using Insight Predict to rank the documents most likely to be hot, we were able to bring a higher concentration of them to the front of the review queue. Then, using Predict's automated workflow, we fed these ranked documents to the review attorneys. Reviewers coded documents in small batches of 20, in order to take maximum advantage of Predict's seamless continuous active learning. Each completed batch triggered new ranking rounds in the background (each running in under 10 minutes), such that dozens of rounds were run every day to integrate new review feedback and improve the next batches of documents served on-demand to the review team.

For the batches being fed to the reviewers, Predict quickly raised the richness of hot documents from 1% to 7%. That meant that the reviewers were getting seven times the richness they would otherwise have seen.

It also meant that they were able to find the majority of hot documents after reviewing only 8% of the collection. To understand this, compare these two graphs. The first shows the hot documents distributed randomly throughout the population:

This second graph shows the hot documents as ranked by Predict. The area shaded grey represents the last point we measured during this review. At that point, the attorneys had identified about 70% of the total predicted number of hot documents, but had reviewed only 8% of the produced population:

This flux curve further illustrates Predict's ability to adjust to distinct events during the course of the review, such as the arrival of new productions and the arrival of new, untrained reviewers.

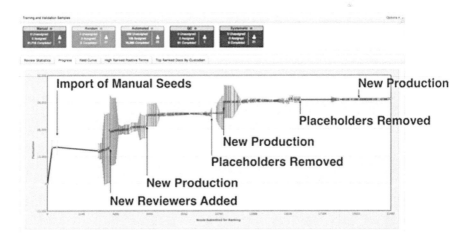

Contextual Diversity vs. 'Hide the Ball'

One other feature of Predict that proved important in this case was its ability to perform contextual diversity sampling. Predict is the only TAR tool on the market with this ability. It samples the population to ensure that there are no significant threads or pockets of documents that escape human review, even when a large proportion of the population will not have attorney eyes on it.

This has a significant benefit in a case such as this, where a plaintiff of limited means is up against a Goliath of a defendant. A common story in such cases has the defendant trying to bury revealing or damaging documents within a large, late production. When this happened during a traditional manual review, the documents might not have been noticed for some time.

However, with Predict's contextual diversity engine re-ranking and analyzing the entire document set every time, a pocket of new documents unlike anything reviewers have seen before is immediately recognized, and exemplars from those new pockets will be pulled as contextual diversity seeds and put in front of reviewers in the very next batch of documents to be reviewed.

The Bottom Line

These plaintiffs lacked the resources to engage in a brute-force review of the defendant's large, rolling productions. Insight Predict gave them the ability to quickly find the majority of hot documents and reduce the overall number of documents they had to review by more than 90%.

20

Case Study: TAR Does Double Duty in a Government Probe

Insight Predict Reduces Review and Rescues Privileged Documents

In a highly sensitive government investigation, discovery is a delicate balancing act. You want to be sure to produce everything you are supposed to produce. But you just as surely want to steer clear of inadvertently producing privileged information. On both sides of this equation, technology assisted review (TAR) can provide greater certainty, while still reducing the overall time and cost of your review.

This was demonstrated in a case involving a government investigation of a digital entertainment company. Using Insight Predict, Catalyst's advanced TAR platform, the company's legal team achieved two critical outcomes. First, even though they wanted eyes-on review of every document that might be produced, they still were able to stop after reviewing just 60% of the total population. Second, by using Predict as a pre-production check for privileged documents, they "rescued" several privileged documents that had been slated for production.

Challenge: Review Carefully but Control Time and Cost

This government investigation required review of about 60,000 documents. Although the document population was relatively small, the case was highly sensitive. For that reason, the legal team wanted to manually review every document that might go out the door, including not only responsive documents, but also family members of those documents that were likely unresponsive.

At the same time, the team wanted to keep the time and cost of the review as low as possible. And they wanted to be extremely careful to avoid inadvertently producing any privileged information.

Solution: Use Insight Predict to Cut Review and Rescue Privileged Docs

The initial sample of the document population found it to have 20% richness. But after the team reviewed a few hundred seed documents, Predict was able to increase fourfold—to 80%—the richness of the documents that it was automatically queuing up for the review team.

Further, despite the legal team's thorough approach of reviewing every potentially responsive document, Predict enabled them to stop the review just 60% through the total population yet still achieve nearly 96% recall. That means they were able to defensibly cut 40% of the human-reviewable population while still achieving a measured recall well above the theoretical limit for full-scale human review.

The yield curve from the case shows a nearly

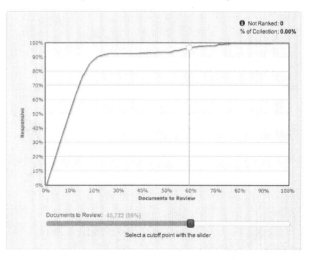

perfect ranking for a 20% rich population at first. It is almost a straight line until we reach about 80% recall. Then it starts to flatten out, indicating that we are running out of responsive documents. The shaded line shows a cutoff selected at the 60% mark, resulting in recall (or "yield") of about 96% of all relevant documents in the population.

Using Predict as a Check for Privileged Documents

A few days before production, we noticed that the legal team had started privilege review. They had already reviewed and QC'd several hundred potentially privileged documents. We suggested that we create an additional Predict ranking for privilege. We would use the documents already coded for privilege as training seeds, and then rank the whole population based on likelihood of being privileged.

This process took about an hour. Once it was done, we batched the top 100 documents that Predict identified as potentially privileged but that reviewers had marked as responsive for production. When the legal team reviewed this batch, they found five privileged documents that would have been produced if not for Predict.

We continued the process several more times that same day, batching documents further down the ranked list. Two more privileged documents were quickly found. After about 500 documents, the technique stopped yielding additional mismarked documents and a safe stopping point had been reached. In all, this process rescued seven privileged documents that would otherwise have been produced.

The Bottom Line

In this case, Insight Predict not only cut the time and cost of the review, but it also served as a critical check and balance on the process. It enabled the company's legal team to eliminate 40% of the document population from eyes-on review yet still be highly confident of the thoroughness of the production. At the same time, Predict provided a safety net that prevented the inadvertent production of privileged documents.

Suggested Reading on TAR

Great Articles on Search and Technology Assisted Review

- Maura R. Grossman & Gordon V. Cormack, *Technology-Assisted Review Can Be More Effective and More Efficient Than Exhaustive Manual Review*, XVII Rich. J.L. & Tech. 11 (2011), http://jolt.richmond.edu/v17i3/article11.pdf

- Maura R. Grossman & Gordon V. Cormack, *Inconsistent Responsiveness Determination in Document Review: Difference of Opinion or Human Error?*, 32 Pace L. Rev. 267 (2012), http://digitalcommons.pace.edu/plr/vol32/iss2/

- Herbert Roitblatt, *Measurement in eDiscovery*, http://www.theolp.org/Resources/Documents/Measurement%20in%20eDiscovery%20-%20Herb%20Roitblat.pdf (2013)

- Karl Schieneman and Thomas Gricks, *The Implications of Rule 26(g) on the Use of Technology-Assisted Review*, Federal Courts Law Review, Vol. 7, Issue 1, http://www.fclr.org/fclr/articles/html/2010/Gricks.pdf (2013)

- Gordon V. Cormack & Maura R. Grossman, *Evaluation of Machine Learning Protocols for Technology-Assisted Review in Electronic Discovery*, in Proceedings of the 37th International ACM SIGIR Conference on Research and Development in Information Retrieval (SIGIR '14) (July 2014), at 153-62, http://dx.doi.org/10.1145/2600428.2609601

- Maura R. Grossman & Gordon V. Cormack, Comments on *"The Implications of Rule 26(g) on the Use of Technology-Assisted Review,"* 7 Fed. Courts L. Rev. 285 (2014), http://www.fclr.org/fclr/articles/pdf/comments-implications-rule26g-tar-62314.pdf

- Maura R. Grossman & Gordon V. Cormack, *The Grossman-Cormack Glossary of Technology-Assisted Review with Foreword by John M. Facciola*, U.S. Magistrate Judge, 7 Fed. Courts L. Rev. 1 (2013), http://www.fclr.org/fclr/articles/html/2010/grossman.pdf

Not to Be Missed Blogs and Web Sites Covering Search, Analytics and Technology Assisted Review

- *Catalyst E-Discovery Search Blog*, http://www.catalystsecure.com/blog.

- *e-Discovery Team* (Ralph Losey), http://e-discoveryteam.com

- *Clustify Blog* (William Dimm), http://blog.cluster-text.com/author/bdimm/

- *Ball in Your Court* (Craig Ball), https://ballinyourcourt.wordpress.com/

- *ESI Bytes* (podcasts worth hearing from Karl Scheineman), http://esibytes.com/category/blog/category-4/

- *Ride the Lightning* (Sharon D. Nelson), http://ridethelightning.senseient.com

Appendix A

TAR in the Courts

A Compendium of Case Law About Technology Assisted Review

It is four years since the first court decision approving the use of technology assisted review in e-discovery. "Counsel no longer have to worry about being the 'first' or 'guinea pig' for judicial acceptance of computer-assisted review," U.S. Magistrate Judge Andrew J. Peck declared in his groundbreaking opinion in Da Silva Moore v. Publicis Groupe.

Judge Peck did not open a floodgate of judicial decisions on TAR. To date, there have been less than 30 such decisions and not one from an appellate court.

However, what he did do—just as he said—was to set the stage for judicial acceptance of TAR. Not a single court since has questioned the soundness of Judge Peck's decision. To the contrary, courts uniformly cite his ruling with approval.

That does not mean that every court orders TAR in every case. The one overarching lesson of the TAR decisions to date is that each case stands on its own merits. Courts look not only to the efficiency and effectiveness of TAR, but also to issues of proportionality and cooperation.

What follows is a summary of the cases to date involving TAR.

2012

***Da Silva Moore, et al. v. Publicis Groupe*, No. 11 Civ. 1279 (ALC)(AJP), 2012 WL 607412 (S.D.N.Y. Feb. 24, 2012).**

Judge: U.S. Magistrate Judge Andrew J. Peck

Holding: The court formally approved the use of TAR to locate responsive documents. The court also held that Federal Rule of Evidence 702 and the Daubert standard for the admissibility of expert testimony do not apply to discovery search methods.

Significance: This is the first judicial opinion approving the use of TAR in e-discovery.

Notable quote: *"What the Bar should take away from this Opinion is that computer-assisted review is an available tool and should be seriously considered for use in large-data-volume cases where it may save the producing party (or both parties) significant amounts of legal fees in document review. Counsel no longer have to worry about being the 'first' or 'guinea pig' for judicial acceptance of computer-assisted review."*

***Global Aerospace, Inc. v. Landow Aviation, L.P.*, No. CL 61040 (Vir. Cir. Ct. Apr. 23, 2012).**

Judge: Circuit Judge James H. Chamblin

Holding: Despite plaintiffs' objection, court ordered that defendants may use predictive coding for the purposes of processing and producing ESI, without prejudice to plaintiffs later raising issues as to the completeness of the production or the ongoing use of predictive coding.

Significance: This appears to be the first state court case expressly approving the use of TAR.

Notable quote: *"Defendants shall be allowed to proceed with the use of predictive coding for purposes of the processing and production of electronically stored information."*

Da Silva Moore, et al. v. Publicis Groupe, 2012 WL 1446534 (S.D.N.Y. Apr. 26, 2012).

Judge: U.S. District Judge Andrew L. Carter Jr.

Holding: The court affirmed Magistrate Judge Peck's order approving the use of TAR.

Significance: Insofar as Judge Peck's order was the first judicial opinion approving the use of TAR, its affirmance by Judge Carter further cemented its significance.

Notable quote: *"Judge Peck concluded that under the circumstances of this particular case, the use of the predictive coding software as specified in the ESI protocol is more appropriate than keyword searching. The court does not find a basis to hold that his conclusion is clearly erroneous or contrary to law."*

Nat'l Day Laborer Org. Network v. U.S. Immigration & Customs Enforcement Agency, No. 10 Civ. 2488 (SAS), 2012 WL 2878130 (S.D.N.Y. July 13, 2012).

Judge: U.S. District Judge Shira Scheindlin

Holding: In an action under the federal Freedom of Information Act, the court held that the federal government's searches for responsive documents were inadequate because of their failure to properly employ modern search technologies.

Significance: In a decision in which Judge Scheindlin urged the government to "learn to use twenty-first century technologies," she discussed predictive coding as representative of "emerging best practices" in compensating for the shortcomings of simple keyword search.

Notable quote: *"Beyond the use of keyword search, parties can (and frequently should) rely on latent semantic indexing, statistical probability models, and machine learning tools to find responsive documents. Through iterative learning, these methods (known as 'computer-assisted' or 'predictive' coding) allow humans to teach computers what documents are and are not responsive to a particular FOIA or discovery request and they can significantly increase the effectiveness and efficiency of searches."*

In re Actos (Pioglitazone) Prods. Liab. Litig., **MDL No. 6:11-MD-2299 (W.D. La. July 27, 2012).**

Judge: Magistrate Judge Patrick J. Hanna

Holding: In a multi-district products liability matter, the magistrate judge approved the parties' agreement to use TAR for the production of ESI.

Significance: This case was significant as one of the earliest in which a federal court explicitly endorsed the use of TAR.

Notable quote: None.

EORHB, Inc. v. HOA Holdings, LLC, **No. 7409-VCL (Del. Ch. Oct. 15, 2012).**

Judge: Vice Chancellor J. Travis Laster

Holding: Court on its own initiative ordered parties to use predictive coding or to show cause why they should not.

Significance: This was another early case in which the judge acknowledged the efficacy of using TAR.

Notable quote: *"This seems to me to be an ideal non-expedited case in which the parties would benefit from using predictive coding. I would like you all, if you do not want to use predictive coding, to show cause why this is not a case where predictive coding is the way to go."*

2013

***Gabriel Techs., Corp. v. Qualcomm, Inc.*, No. 08CV1992 AJB (MDD), 2013 WL 410103 (S.D. Cal. Feb. 1, 2013).**

Judge: U.S. District Judge Anthony J. Battaglia

Holding: Following entry of judgment in their favor in a patent infringement case, defendants filed a motion seeking attorneys' fees, including $2.8 million "attributable to computer-assisted, algorithm-driven document review." The court found that amount to be reasonable and approved it.

Significance: The court found that the costs of TAR could be recovered as part of the costs and attorneys' fees awarded to the prevailing party in patent litigation.

Notable quote: *"[T]he Court finds [lead counsel] Cooley's decision to undertake a more efficient and less time-consuming method of document review to be reasonable under the circumstances. In this case, the nature of the Plaintiffs' claims resulted in significant discovery and document production, and Cooley seemingly reduced the overall fees and attorney hours required by performing electronic document review at the outset. Thus, the Court finds the requested amount of $2,829,349.10 to be reasonable."*

***Cambridge Place Inv. Mgmt, Inc. v. Morgan Stanley*, No. SUCV2010-2741 (Mass. Super. Ct. Suffolk Mar. 21, 2013).**

Judge: Superior Court Judge Thomas P. Billings

Holding: Court approving the use of TAR over the objection of the opposing party.

Significance: It was notable that the court approved the use of TAR over the opposing party's objection.

Notable Quote: None.

Edwards v. Nat'l Milk Producers Federation, No. 3:11-cv-04766 (N.D. Cal., Apr. 17, 2013).

Judge: U.S. District Judge Jeffrey S. White.

Holding: Court entered order approving the parties stipulated protocol for the use of TAR.

Significance: The judge accepted the parties' stipulation to use a TAR protocol.

Notable Quote: None.

In re Biomet M2a Magnum Hip Implant Prods. Liab. Litig., 2013 U.S. Dist. LEXIS 84440 (N.D. Ind. Apr. 18, 2013).

Judge: U.S. District Judge Robert L. Miller Jr.

Holding: Court held that defendant's use of keyword searching to cull documents population prior to application of TAR was reasonable under the requirements of Federal Rules of Civil Procedure 26(b). It declined to require the defendant to go back and use TAR on the entire ESI population.

Significance: The court found that proportionality trumped purity, and that even if predictive coding might unearth additional relevant documents, the cost would far outweigh the likely benefits.

Notable quote: *"It might well be that predictive coding, instead of a keyword search, at Stage Two of the process would unearth additional relevant documents. But it would cost Biomet a million, or millions, of dollars to test the Steering Committee's theory that predictive coding would produce a significantly greater number of relevant documents. Even in light of the* *needs of the hundreds of plaintiffs in this case, the very large amount in controversy, the parties' resources, the importance of the issues at stake, and the importance of this discovery in resolving the issues, I can't find that the likely benefits of the discovery proposed by the Steering Committee equals or outweighs its additional burden on, and additional expense to, Biomet."*

EORHB, Inc. v. HOA Holdings, LLC, No. 7409-VCL, 2013 WL 1960621 (Del. Ch. May 6, 2013).

Judge: Vice Chancellor J. Travis Laster.

Holding: In an earlier order, the court ordered the parties to "retain a single discovery vendor to be used by both sides" and to "conduct document review with the assistance of predictive coding." In this new order, the court accepted the parties' agreement that defendants could use TAR and retain their own vendor and that plaintiffs would not be required to use TAR because the cost would likely outweigh the benefit.

Significance: The court declined to require a party to use TAR when its cost would outweigh its anticipated benefit.

Notable quote: *"[B]ased on the low volume of relevant documents expected to be produced in discovery by [plaintiffs], the cost of using predictive coding assistance would likely be outweighed by any practical benefit of its use."*

Gordon v. Kaleida Health, No. 08-CV-378S(F), 2013 WL 2250579 (W.D.N.Y. May 21, 2013).

Judge: U.S. Magistrate Judge Leslie G. Foschio.

Holding: Impatient with the parties' year-long attempts to agree on how to achieve a cost-effective review of some 200,000-300,000 emails, the magistrate judge suggested they try predictive coding. That led to a dispute over the extent to which the parties should meet and confer in order to agree on a TAR protocol. Because the parties ultimately agreed to meet, the judge never decided any substantive TAR issue.

Significance: The significance of this case is that it was the judge, not the litigants, who suggested the use of predictive coding.

Notable quote: *"At the last of a series of ESI discovery status conferences with the court, ... the court expressed dissatisfaction with the parties' lack of progress toward resolving issues related to completion of review and production of Defendants' e-mails using the key-word search method, and pointed to the availability of predictive coding, a computer assisted ESI reviewing and production method, directing the parties' attention to the recent decision of Magistrate Judge Peck in Moore v. Publicis Groupe & MSL Group, 287 F.R.D. 182 (S.D.N.Y. 2012), approving use of predictive coding in a case involving over 3 million e-mails."*

In re Biomet M2a Magnum Hip Implant Prods. Liab. Litig., 2013 U.S. Dist. LEXIS 172570 (N.D. Ind. Aug. 21, 2013).

Judge: U.S. District Judge Robert L. Miller Jr.

Holding: The court ruled that defendants need not identify which of the documents, from among those they had already produced, were used in the training of the defendants' TAR algorithm.

Significance: Because defendants had already complied with their obligation under the FRCP to produce relevant documents, the court held that it had no authority to compel the defendants to identify the specific documents it had used as seeds. Even so, the court said that it was troubled by the defendants' lack of cooperation.

Notable quote: *"The Steering Committee knows of the existence and location of each discoverable document Biomet used in the seed set: those documents have been disclosed to the Steering Committee. The Steering Committee wants to know, not whether a document exists or where it is, but rather how Biomet used certain documents before disclosing them. Rule 26(b)(1) doesn't make such information disclosable."*

2014

Federal Housing Finance Agency v. HSBC North America Holdings, 2014 WL 584300 (S.D.N.Y. Feb. 14, 2014).

Judge: U.S. District Judge Denise Cote

Holding: In a memorandum opinion, the judge stated that, earlier in the discovery process, she had permitted one defendant, JPMorgan Chase, to use predictive coding over the plaintiff's objection. She recounted this in making the point that discovery is not expected to be a perfect process, but one in which parties act with diligence and good faith.

Significance: The case is significant as another in which a federal court allowed the use of TAR. It is also significant for its recognition that discovery does not require perfection.

Notable quote: *"Parties in litigation are required to be diligent and to act in good faith in producing documents in discovery. The production of documents in litigation such as this is a herculean undertaking, requiring an army of personnel and the production of an extraordinary volume of documents. Clients pay counsel vast sums of money in the course of this undertaking, both to produce documents and to review documents received from others. Despite the commitment of these resources, no one could or should expect perfection from this process. All that can be legitimately expected is a good faith, diligent commitment to produce all responsive documents uncovered when following the protocols to which the parties have agreed, or which a court has ordered."*

Aurora Cooperative Elevator Co. v. Aventine Renewable Energy - Aurora West LLC, 12 Civ. 0230, Dkt. No 147 (D. Neb. Mar. 10, 2014).

Judge: U.S. Magistrate Judge Cheryl Zwart.

Holding: Court granted plaintiff's motion to compel the use of TAR.

Significance: Over defendant's objection, the court granted plaintiff's request to compel the use of TAR.

Notable Quote: *"For at least this first discovery stage, the parties shall consult with a computer forensic expert to create search protocols, including predictive coding as needed, for a computerized review of the parties' electronic records."*

Progressive Cas. Ins. Co. v. Delaney, No. 2:11-cv-00678-LRH-PAL, 2014 WL 2112927 (D. Nev. May 20, 2014).

Judge: U.S. Magistrate Judge Peggy A. Leen.

Holding: The court rejected a party's unilateral decision to use TAR because the party had already demonstrated that it lacked the willingness to engage in the type of cooperation and transparency that is needed for a TAR protocol to be accepted by a court.

Significance: The case is a reminder that efficiency and cost-effectiveness are not the only factors a court will look at in evaluating the use of TAR. Cooperation and transparency are also important factors.

Notable quote: *"The cases which have approved technology assisted review of ESI have required an unprecedented degree of transparency and cooperation among counsel in the review and production of ESI responsive to discovery requests."*

FDIC v. Bowden, No. CV413-245, 2014 WL 2548137 (S.D. Ga. June 6, 2014).

Judge: Magistrate Judge G.R. Smith

Holding: In case involving some 2.01 terabytes of data, or 153.6 million pages of documents, the court suggested that the parties consider using TAR.

Significance: The court recognized TAR is more accurate than human review or keyword searching.

Notable quote: *"Predictive coding has emerged as a far more accurate* *means of producing responsive ESI in discovery. Studies show it is far more accurate than human review or keyword searches which have their own limitations." (Quoting <u>Progressive Cas. Ins. Co. v. Delaney</u>, 2014 WL 2112927 at *8 (D. Nev. May 20, 2014)).*

Indep. Living Ctr. of S. Cal. v. City of Los Angeles, 2:12-cv-00551 (C.D. Cal. June 26, 2014).

Judge: U.S. Magistrate Judge Patrick J. Walsh.

Holding: The court ordered defendant to use TAR to review more than 2 million documents. In response to plaintiff's insistence that the TAR protocol include a quality assurance phase, the court ordered plaintiff to pay half the cost of the quality assurance phase.

Significance: The court declined to perform a cost-shifting analysis before requiring plaintiff to pay half the cost of QC.

Notable Quote: *"The quality assurance step is part of a program that the Court ordered the City to buy for $50,000 and use in this case. It is a feature that does not exist in traditional production, i.e., reviewing the documents and producing them to the other side. Nor is it a feature in key word searches, the method Plaintiffs were championing when the Court became involved and ordered the City to use predictive coding. It is a feature available in predictive coding which quantifies the level of accuracy in the search. The fact that it exists in the system does not mean that the City has to employ it and pay for it. If Plaintiffs truly believe that quality assurance step is important, they should pay for employing it by splitting the costs with the City."*

Bridgestone Americas, Inc. v. Int. Bus. Machs. Corp., No. 3:13-1196 **(M.D. Tenn. July 22, 2014).**

Judge: U.S. Magistrate Judge Joe B. Brown.

Holding: The court approved the plaintiff's request to use predictive coding to review over 2 million documents, over defendant's objections that the request was an unwarranted change in the original case management order and that it would be unfair to use predictive coding after an initial screening has been done with search terms.

Significance: The opinion suggests that e-discovery should be a fluid and transparent process and that principles of efficiency and proportionality may justify a party to "switch horses in midstream," as the magistrate judge wrote.

Notable quote: *"In the final analysis, the use of predictive coding is a judgment call, hopefully keeping in mind the exhortation of Rule 26 that discovery be tailored by the court to be as efficient and cost-effective as possible. In this case, we are talking about millions of documents to be reviewed with costs likewise in the millions. There is no single, simple, correct solution possible under these circumstances."*

In re Bridgepoint Educ., **No. 12cv1737 JM (JLB), 2014 WL 3867495 (S.D. Cal. Aug. 6, 2014).**

Judge: Magistrate Judge Jill L. Burkhardt.

Holding: This brief order included two holdings pertaining to TAR. First, in declining plaintiffs' request to expand the scope of discovery as unduly burdensome on defendants, the court rejected plaintiffs' argument that the use of predictive coding would alleviate any added burden. Second, the court declined to order defendants to use predictive coding for documents they had already produced, reasoning that it had approved defendants' method of "using linear screening with the aid of search terms."

Significance: The court applied principles of proportionality to limit the scope of discovery and the use of TAR.

Notable quote: "Defendants argued that putting the Individual Defendant documents already screened through predictive coding is likely to negatively impact the reliability of the predictive coding process. Defendants suggested that they would be willing to run additional search terms for the documents already screened but were not amenable to running these documents through the predictive coding process."

Dynamo Holdings Ltd. P'ship v. Comm'r of Internal Revenue, Nos. 2685-11, 8393-12 (T.C. Sept. 17, 2014).

Judge: U.S. Tax Court Judge Ronald L. Buch

Holding: The Tax Court approved petitioner's use of TAR to identify potentially responsive and privileged data contained on two backup tapes, despite respondent's objection that the technology was unproven.

Significance: This is the first opinion to formally sanction the use of TAR in the Tax Court.

Notable quote: *"Although predictive coding is a relatively new technique, and a technique that has yet to be sanctioned (let alone mentioned) by this Court in a published Opinion, the understanding of e-discovery and electronic media has advanced significantly in the last few years, thus making predictive coding more acceptable in the technology industry than it may have previously been. In fact, we understand that the technology industry now considers predictive coding to be widely accepted for limiting e-discovery to relevant documents and effecting discovery of ESI without an undue burden."*

2015

Chevron Corp. v. Snaider, No. 14-cv-01354-RBJ-KMT, 2015 WL 226110 (D. Col. Jan. 15, 2015).

Judge: U.S. Magistrate Judge Kathleen M. Tafoya

Holding: In multi-national dispute, court declines to quash discovery subpoena where defendant failed to prove that compliance with the subpoena would subject him to undue burden or expense, in part because he failed to address the likelihood that TAR could be used to reduce the cost of review.

Significance: The court recognized that TAR can significantly reduce the cost of review and that a claim of undue burden should take that into account.

Notable Quote: *"Snaider does not address the likelihood that in a case such as this computer-assisted review would no doubt be invoked, and while that is costly, it is much more efficient than assigning individuals to review a large volume of paperwork."*

Connecticut Gen. Life Ins. Co. v. Health Diagnostic Lab., Inc., No. 3:14-cv-01519, 2015 WL 417120 (D. Conn. Jan. 28, 2015).

Judge: U.S. District Judge Victor A. Bolden

Holding: Court approved e-discovery stipulation that said that if a party chooses to use TAR, it need not "share the intricacies" of the methodology unless there is a good faith allegation of a violation of Rule 26.

Significance: The degree of transparency required when parties use TAR remains an open question in the courts. Here, the judge approved a stipulation limiting disclosure about "the intricacies" of the TAR methodology unless there was a good faith allegation of a violation of Rule 26.

Notable Quote: *"To the extent that a Party chooses to search and review using a technology or methodology other than search terms (including, for instance, predictive coding), that Party shall disclose its intent to use that technology and the name of the review tool. However, the Party need not share the intricacies of said methodology unless and until there is a good faith allegation of a violation of Rule 26."*

Rio Tinto PLC v. Vale SA, Case 1:14-cv-03042-RMB-AJP (S.D. N.Y. March 3, 2015).

Judge: U.S. Magistrate Judge Andrew J. Peck.

Holding: The court approved the parties' stipulated protocol for technology assisted review.

Significance: The opinion is significant for several reasons. For one, it explicitly recognizes that TAR has become so widely accepted that courts would approve its use as a matter of "black letter law." For another, the opinion acknowledges that the extent of litigants' obligation to be transparent and to cooperate in the use of TAR remains an open question, particularly with regard to whether all the documents used in the seed set must be shared with the opposing party. Notably, however, the court recognized that the transparency issue disappears or diminishes if the TAR methodology uses Continuous Active Learning, where the seed set is unnecessary or less significant.

Notable quote: *"In the three years since Da Silva Moore, the case law has developed to the point that it is now black letter law that where the producing party wants to utilize TAR for document review, courts will permit it."*

Malone v. Kantner Ingredients, Inc., 2015 WL 1470334 (D. Neb. Mar. 31, 2015).

Judge: U.S. Magistrate Judge Cheryl R. Zwart

Holding: After plaintiffs' forensics expert found responsive documents that the defendant had not previously disclosed, plaintiffs brought a motion to penalize defendants for failing to produce all responsive documents and to require defendants to reimburse them for the cost of the expert's work. The judge ruled that plaintiffs' allegations did not justify the reimbursement they requested, in that all plaintiffs had alleged was that the defendants made a mistake in their own review, and mistakes are bound to happen in manual review.

Significance: The case is significant for reaffirming that the discovery standard is reasonableness, not perfection, and for recognizing that TAR is not only more efficient and cost-effective than human review, but also more accurate.

Notable Quote: *"Predictive coding is now promoted (and gaining acceptance) as not only a more efficient and cost effective method of ESI* review, but a more accurate one. Nicholas Barry, Man Versus Machine Review: The Showdown Between Hordes of Discovery Lawyers and A Computer-Utilizing Predictive-Coding Technology, 15 Vand. J. Ent. & Tech. L. 343 (2013); Maura R. Grossman & Gordon V. Cormack, Technology-Assisted Review in E-Discovery Can Be More Effective and More Efficient Than Exhaustive Manual Review, 17 Rich. J.L. & Tech. 11, P 5 (2011)."

Rio Tinto PLC v. Vale S.A., 14 Civ. 3042 (RMB)(AJP) (S.D. N.Y. July 15, 2015).

Judge: U.S. Magistrate Judge Andrew J. Peck.

Holding: The court approved defendant's application to appoint Maura Grossman as a special master to assist with issues concerning TAR.

Significance: Plaintiff objected to the appointment on the ground that it should have been made much earlier in the case, when there remained more significant TAR issues. Although the court agreed that an earlier appointment would have been preferable, it found that there were still unresolved issues concerning TAR about which Ms. Grossman's expertise would be helpful. Plaintiff also objected on the ground that one of defendant's lawyers had prior conversations about TAR with Ms. Grossman in connection with her volunteer work for The Sedona Conference and in seeking general information about TAR. The court found that these conversations provided no basis to disqualify Ms. Grossman.

Notable Quote: *"Rio Tinto further objects because one of Vale's lawyers had three conversations with Ms. Grossman about TAR issues. The Court does not believe that the contact in connection with The Sedona Conference should or does prevent Ms. Grossman from serving as special master. We should be encouraging, not discouraging, participation in Bar associations and similar organizations. The other two conversations were general, requesting sources of information from Ms. Grossman, and in my opinion Ms. Grossman should be applauded for her willingness to share her expertise with others. We should remember that the law is still a learned profession."*

Knauf Insulation LLC v. Johns Manville Corporation, No. 1:15-cv-00111-WTL-MJD (S.D. Ind. Nov. 13, 2015).

Judge: U.S. Magistrate Judge Mark J. Dinsmore

Holding: Defendant sought to limit the number of custodians subject to discovery, arguing in part that it would facilitate the TAR process. The judge denied the request, holding that the potential benefit to the plaintiff of including those custodians outweighed the additional cost.

Significance: Even though the defendant argued that limiting custodians would facilitate the TAR process, the judge found that the potential benefit to the plaintiff outweighed the additional cost to the defendants.

Notable Quote: *"[I]n the realm of electronic discovery there are no guarantees that every relevant responsive document will be found. Even in the best case scenario, the process likely will not yield 100 percent production of all relevant material. But how many relevant responsive documents are too many to voluntarily walk away from? As Knauf pointed out, JM's proposal would guarantee a zero percent recall for the 28 custodians not chosen. There is no way to predict how many non-duplicate relevant emails may be in the possession of those 28 custodians; individuals that JM itself identified as likely to possess relevant information. ... [T]here is no evidence to help the Court weigh how likely it is that ESI from the 28 tangential custodians would yield information relevant to the issues in this litigation. However, in a high value case such as this one, the burden of the additional $18,000 expense does not outweigh the potential benefit to Knauf of receiving those emails."*

About Catalyst

Catalyst designs, hosts and services the world's fastest and most powerful document repositories for large-scale discovery and regulatory compliance. For over fifteen years, corporations and their counsel have relied on Catalyst to help reduce litigation costs and take control of complex legal matters. As a technology platform company, our mission is to create software clients can use to manage large document repositories from raw files through search, analysis, review and production.

We also provide professional services to help clients get the most out of our software and manage their information governance and discovery tasks with maximum efficiency.

To learn more about Technology Assisted Review and Catalyst, visit
www.catalystsecure.com or call 877.557.4273

To download the digital edition of the book, visit
www.catalystsecure.com/TARforSmartPeople